Cooking the West Indian Way

Cooking the West Indian Way

Dalton Babb

CARIBBEAN

Macmillan Education
Between Towns Road, Oxford OX4 3PP
A division of Macmillan Publishers Limited
Companies and representatives throughout the world

www.macmillan-caribbean.com

ISBN 978 0 333 42829 0

Text © Dalton Babb 1986

First published 1986

Printed in Malaysia

2010   2009   2008   2007
20   19   18   17   16   15

Contents

Foreword

This is the fourth cook book by Dalton Babb and the second edition of the one titled *'Cooking The West Indian Way'*. The first two were published under the title *'Cooking the Caribbean Way'*.

This edition has in it many of Babb's old recipes but there are a host of new ones which attest to the thought and imagination which Dalton Babb has always put into his cooking. In fact, although self-taught, he is clearly a master of the culinary art to which he has brought a West Indian flavour.

Once again this book is dedicated to Mrs. Eileen Robinson, proprietress of the small but famous Bagshot House Hotel on the St. Lawrence coast in the island of Barbados. It was there that Dalton Babb, after arriving from his native St. Vincent, in the chain of islands forming the eastern border of the Caribbean sea, was first able to give full range to his talents, and to learn from the many guests from North America and Europe who stayed there, what visitors really appreciate about West Indian cooking. Such visitors included famous people like the late author Nicholas Montserrat who always stayed at Bagshot House on his many visits to Barbados, enticed back by its informal atmosphere and Babb's cooking.

Subsequently Dalton Babb became chef and housekeeper for Lord and Lady Rothschild running the household at their winter home on the Sandy Lane Estate both while they were in residence and when they were back in England for spring, summer or autumn. It was here that he met Donald M. Kendall, then President of the Pepsi Cola Company who later employed him at his home in New York and followed this up by appointing him to run the Executive Dining Room at Pepsi Cola.

As with the third edition, a special buffet luncheon party was given by Mrs. Robinson at Bagshot House to launch this edition with the meal prepared, supervised and served by Dalton Babb. The cover picture and others on inside pages showing the beach and interior at Bagshot House in the background were taken by Carrington Photo Creations Ltd. at the luncheon party. It was another memorable day for gourmets at Bagshot House.

Trevor Gale
Editor: *Bajan Magazine*

Oven temperatures

Electric Setting	Gas Mark
225°F – 110°C	$\frac{1}{4}$
250°F – 130°C	$\frac{1}{2}$
275°F – 140°C	1
300°F – 150°C	2
325°F – 170°C	3
350°F – 180°C	4
375°F – 190°C	5
400°F – 200°C	6
425°F – 220°C	7
450°F – 230°C	8
475°F – 240°C	9

Measures

1 dash	$\frac{1}{6}$ teaspoon
1 teaspoon	$\frac{1}{8}$ ounce
1 tablespoon	3 teaspoons
1 glass (wineglass)	4 ounces
1 pint	$2\frac{1}{2}$ U.S. cups

Note: The term half and half in some recipes refers to a mixture of cream and whole milk.

1 Soups

Babb's homemade cucumber soup

4 green peppers (sweet)
4 stalks celery
1 large onion
3 cucumbers

$\frac{1}{4}$ tsp. black pepper
6 packages chicken bouillon
1 tsp. curry powder
1 dash Tabasco sauce

Put all the ingredients in a blender and mix well, then add:

$1\frac{1}{2}$ cups half and half

2 jiggers sherry

Stir mixture gently (if too thick, add more half and half). Put in refrigerator to chill before serving. Just before serving, add 1 tsp. sour cream and chopped parsley.
Serve with hot biscuits and Babb's main course of Southern Fried Chicken.

Babb's homemade papaya soup

1 large papaya
4 sticks carrot
1 small marrow
4 scallions
2 cans evaporated milk

2 jiggers Mount Gay rum
$\frac{1}{4}$ tsp. black pepper
3 packages chicken bouillon
3 packages beef bouillon

Mix the ingredients in a blender then place in refrigerator to chill. Just before serving add 1 tsp. sour cream with chopped chives. Serve with dinner rolls followed by a main course of Flying Fish.

Christmas Jug

(Made from green peas)

Put some pig tails in a saucepan with some finely sliced ham and water and boil for 20 minutes. Meanwhile shell and wash the green peas.
After 20 minutes, put the green peas in saucepan with ham and pig tails. Add the following ingredients:

$\frac{1}{4}$ tsp. thyme
$\frac{1}{4}$ tsp. black pepper
1 onion, chopped fine

When peas are cooked (soft), add $\frac{1}{2}$ stick of butter. Remove tails from saucepan, cut meat off and then replace tails in saucepan. Stir ingredients together and serve.

Babb's special soup for summer

6 large tomatoes	1 jigger sherry
6 stalks celery	$\frac{1}{2}$ jigger A−1 sauce
4 red sweet peppers	$\frac{1}{2}$ bottle ketchup
6 packages of beef bouillon	$\frac{1}{2}$ cup half and half
$\frac{1}{4}$ tsp. black pepper	$\frac{1}{2}$ cup sour cream
$\frac{1}{4}$ tsp. dry thyme	1 carrot, chopped

Blend ingredients in a blender (if too thick, add more half and half), Put in refrigerator to chill. Just before serving put in 1 tsp. sour cream and chopped carrots.
Serve with dinner rolls and Babb's main course of pork chops.

Babb's golden cheese soup

4 oz. margarine
4 oz. flour
1 pt. milk

$1\frac{1}{2}$ pt. chicken stock
4 carrots, grated
10 oz. Cheddar cheese

Make a roux, add stock and milk, stir until thickened. Add grated carrots, simmer for a few minutes. Add grated cheese. Heat until cheese is melted. Garnish with chopped parsley. Serves 10.

Lentil soup from British Guiana

1 cup lentils
3 cups water
$\frac{1}{2}$ cup chopped celery
$\frac{1}{2}$ cup chopped carrots

1 cup chopped tomatoes
2 pork hocks
salt and pepper

Mix all ingredients together in a large pot and simmer slowly for 3−4 hours. Serves 6.

2 Snacks, Appetizers and Drinks

Babb's broiled bacon cheeseburger

(for lunch or dinner)

hamburgers
salt and pepper
4 strips bacon

3 strips American cheese
2 dashes A–1 sauce

Place hamburgers and bacon in broiler, broil until brown. Take out of oven and put on hamburger roll with cheese and seasoning. Serve with Pepsi, iced tea, or white wine.

Babb's asparagus mousse en cocottes

2 15 oz. tins asparagus tips
2 pints chicken stock
$\frac{1}{2}$ pint béchamel sauce (cold)
$\frac{1}{2}$ pint mayonnaise
salt and pepper to taste

$1\frac{1}{2}$ oz. gelatine
$\frac{1}{2}$ pint fresh cream (whipped)
3 egg whites
1 pint aspic jelly

Cut 8 asparagus tips off. Cut in half length ways, put to one side. Put all tender parts of asparagus into blender. Add enough chicken stock

1 level tsp. prepared mustard
1 level tsp. dry mustard
  (Coleman's recommended)

6 slices toast, with crusts
  trimmed off
paprika

Put beer, Worcestershire sauce, mustard and pepper in a glass and let it stand $\frac{1}{2}$ hour or more. Grate cheese (must be grated into thin strips, not cut). Bring beer to a boil over low heat. Add grated cheese, a little at a time. When all the cheese is stirred into the beer, pour over the toast. Sprinkle top with paprika.

Homemade dip from Babb's kitchen

2 tbs. mayonnaise
2 tsp. horseradish sauce
1 bottle Heinz chilli sauce
$\frac{1}{2}$ bottle catsup
1 tbs. A–1 sauce
1 tbs. Worcestershire sauce

2 tsp. Tabasco sauce
$\frac{1}{2}$ tsp. white pepper
1 tsp. extra strong Dijon
  mustard
1 tsp. hollandaise sauce
2 tbs. sugar

Mix thoroughly. Use with any type of chips, or serve mixed in coleslaw or spread in sandwiches.

Pickled pigs' feet from Babb's Manor

6 fresh pigs' feet, halved
6 cups water
2 tsp. salt
1 large cucumber
1 onion, medium size

1 green pepper
3 stalks celery
1 whole hot cherry pepper
juice of 2 limes

Cook pigs' feet in salted water for two hours and place in bowl to cool. Chop all the vegetables very finely, add lime juice and pour over pigs' feet. Let stand at least one half hour before serving, stirring occasionally.
Serve with hot garlic bread and beer.

Stuffed mushrooms

1 dozen medium to large
   mushrooms
1 cup breadcrumbs
4 cloves garlic, finely chopped

$\frac{1}{2}$ cup grated cheese
chopped parsley
olive oil

Combine all ingredients and toss well, adding enough olive oil to moisten mixture slightly. Clean and wash mushrooms and stuff with mixture. Bake in oven for 20 minutes at 350°F.
Serve as an appetizer or vegetable.

Stuffed artichokes appetizer

4 large artichokes
1 cup breadcrumbs
1 tbs. parsley
2 cloves garlic, diced

1 tbs. Parmesan cheese
salt and pepper
1 cup water
2 tbs. olive oil

Wash artichokes and spread leaves out. Mix all dry ingredients, blend well, and fill each leaf with breadcrumb mixture.
In a large skillet, place artichokes standing up and add water to skillet. Pour olive oil on top of each artichoke, cover tightly with lid, and simmer approximately one hour. Serves 4.

Babb's summer soufflé

Combine in saucepan:

2 cups of butter
2 cups of half and half
1$\frac{1}{2}$ cups of flour
8 egg yolks
2 cups grated Cheddar cheese

6 chicken packages bouillon
$\frac{1}{4}$ tsp. black pepper
$\frac{1}{2}$ tsp. thyme
1 tblsp. A–1 sauce
1 small onion, grated

Simmer mixture over low flame and when mixture is cooled, whip 8 egg whites until very stiff and add to mixture. Before ready to bake, add:

$\frac{1}{2}$ lb. ham, cubed
2 red sweet peppers, cut up

Bake at 350°F for $\frac{3}{4}$ hour.
Serve with green tossed salad.

Beverage: Pepsi-Cola

Egg à la Bob

4 soft poached eggs (cold) $\frac{1}{2}$ pt. mayonnaise (curried)
4 oz. cooked rice   1 pimento (Julienne) to garnish
2 oz. French dressing

Season rice. Add French dressing. Arrange on dish. Place eggs onto rice and mask with mayonnaise. Garnish with pimento.

Babb's diet cocktail dip

Cut up green sweet peppers, carrots, fresh broccoli, fresh celery in squares. Cut up cauliflower and radishes in roses. Cut up fresh mushrooms in half. Mix ingredients and add fresh asparagus and green and black olives.

Dip

$\frac{1}{2}$ pint sour cream
1 tsp. dry chives
2 packages chicken bouillon

Mix all ingredients in small bowl. Place diet cocktail vegetables around it.

Frozen daiquiri

(Babb's special summer drink from Bagshot house)

3 jiggers Mount Gay Refined
　Eclipse Barbados rum
1 jigger syrup (mix 2 lb. sugar
　with 1½ cups water, and use
　as needed)

1 jigger lime juice (squeeze
　1 dozen fresh limes)
4 cups ice cubes.

Put all ingredients in blender for approximately 4 minutes. Serve in tall glasses with two straws. Serves 6.

Babb's special titbits

Sprinkle shredded American cheese on top of Doritos corn chips. Add a dash of tabasco. Put under broiler until bubbly.

Planter's punch

2 jiggers of gin, vodka, or
　Scotch
1 jigger syrup (mix 2 lb. sugar
　with 1½ cups water and use as
　needed)
1 jigger lime juice (squeeze
　12 fresh limes)

½ jigger cherry juice
Dash Angostura bitters
4 cups ice cubes

Put all ingredients in blender for approximately 4 minutes. Pour into tall glasses. Add 1 slice banana, 2 slices orange, 1 cherry, and 2 sprigs fresh mint to each glass.

Babb's spicy dip

16 oz. sour cream
1 tsp. mustard
$\frac{1}{4}$ tsp. curry powder

$\frac{1}{4}$ tsp. tabasco
1 heaped tblsp. chopped chives

Mix these ingredients, and serve with Doritos corn chips.

Coconut punch from Babb's Barbados Manor

$2 \times 3\frac{1}{2}$ oz. cans coconut flakes
4 cups milk
$\frac{1}{2}$ cup sugar

2 cups liqueur (any type)
1 tsp. vanilla

Place coconut in a pitcher with 2 cups of milk. Soak for 1 hour. Strain and discard coconut. Add 2 more cups of milk, $\frac{1}{2}$ cup of sugar, 2 cups of liqueur and 1 tsp. vanilla.
Pour 1 cup of mixture into blender. Add 2 cups ice cubes. Blend to liquify until foamy. Combine with reserved milk mixture.
This is a nice summer drink that goes well with Babb's tacos or a cold lunch.

Coffee daiquiri from Cambridge

2 cups coffee
1 cup milk (half and half)
$\frac{1}{2}$ jigger vanilla essence

2 jiggers syrup
1 jigger coffee liqueur
1 jigger dark rum

Mix ingredients in jug. As needed, pour one cup of the mixture and two cups ice cubes into blender and blend.

3 Vegetables and Rice

Stuffed peppers from Toronto

chopped meat
1 large onion
2 stalks celery
$\frac{1}{2}$ tsp. thyme
$\frac{1}{2}$ tsp. black pepper

$\frac{1}{2}$ tsp. garlic salt
1 tblsp. A–1 Sauce
1 tblsp. Worcestershire sauce
chopped up parsley

Sauté ingredients together and add 1 cup cooked rice and stir. Cut top off peppers and clean out.
Put wedge of butter in bottom of each pepper and stuff with meat mixture. Bake in oven at 300°F for 10 minutes.
Serve with dinner rolls, lima beans and mashed potatoes.

Soup: Vegetable soup
Beverage: Ginger ale

Trinidad calalloo

1 head of chopped calalloo or
   romaine lettuce
3 chopped pigs' tails
1 box frozen okra

$\frac{1}{2}$ tsp. Tabasco sauce
$\frac{1}{2}$ tsp. garlic salt
$\frac{1}{2}$ tsp. garlic powder
$\frac{1}{2}$ tsp. dried thyme

2 chopped green peppers
1 chopped large onion
$\frac{1}{2}$ tsp. black pepper

$\frac{1}{2}$ stick butter
1 small can tomato puree

Boil pigs' tails for $\frac{1}{2}$ hour in large saucepan in water and portion of butter. After tails have cooked, add okra and calalloo and boil for an additional 20 minutes. Drain. With remainder of butter, add all other ingredients, mix well and simmer for 10 more minutes. Serves 6. Crabmeat (fresh) can be substituted for pigs' tails.

Vegetable St Lucia

1 lb. eggplant
1 lb. squash
2 large onions
2 green peppers
thyme

salt
pepper
4 oz. oil
1 lb. tomatoes
3 cloves garlic

Peel tomatoes by plunging into boiling water for 1 minute then under cold water. Peel onions and slice. Cut green peppers into thick slices. Cut eggplant and squash into 1″ rounds and tomatoes into quarters. Place in large pan.
Heat oil. Put in onions first. Add green pepper, then squash, and eggplant. Put tomatoes on top. Add thyme and garlic. Add salt and pepper. Cover and simmer for about 1 hour on very low flame. This can be eaten hot or cold. Serves 6-8.

Marinated celery

(from Babb's kitchen)

Cook celery in chicken stock until just tender. Allow to cool. Mix together $\frac{1}{2}$ cup white wine vinegar, $1\frac{1}{2}$ cups oil, pinch of chervil, salt and pepper to taste. Pour over celery and leave in fridge to marinate. Garnish the celery with anchovy fillets and stems of red sweet pepper. Sprinkle with chopped parsley.

Stuffed cucumber

Seed cucumber. Stuff with cream cheese mixed with chopped nuts and chives. Chill. Slice and arrange on bed of lettuce. Mask with mayonnaise. Sprinkle with paprika.

Mushrooms Babb

4–6 oz. button mushrooms
1 large tblsp. olive oil
1 shallot, finely chopped
1 wine glass red wine
1 tsp. chopped fresh thyme

1–2 tblsp. French dressing
   (preferably made with red
   wine vinegar)
salt and pepper

Wash and trim mushrooms (cut off stalks level with caps). Slice stalks length ways and put with mushroom caps. Heat oil in a small frying pan, put in the mushrooms and the shallot. Fry briskly for about 3 minutes, turning and stirring them all the time.
Lift out mushroom mixture with a draining spoon into a bowl. Pour wine into the pan and boil until it is reduced by half. Add to the mushrooms with the herbs and French dressing.
Season well, cover and leave until cold.

Fresh vegetables

2 lbs. fresh string beans
2 packages brussels sprouts
salt

lemon wedges
butter

Boil fresh string beans and brussels sprouts with salt until tender and serve with butter and lemon.

Bagshot House stuffed tomato (Cottage cheese)

8 tomatoes
salt and pepper
4 oz. cottage cheese
1 oz. fresh cream

1 oz. chives or seasoning
  (chopped)
2 oz. French dressing

Skin tomatoes, cut a slice off the top of each. Scoop out seeds and core. Season with salt and pepper. Push cottage cheese through sieve and add cream. Add $\frac{1}{2}$ oz. chives or seasoning. Fill up tomatoes with mixture. Place slice at an angle on top. Spoon a little French dressing over all. Sprinkle with rest of seasoning. Serve cool.

Mushroom cocktail

1 lb. mushrooms
1 large grated onion
3 ozs. olive oil
salt and pepper to taste

2 ozs. brandy
1 oz. lemon juice
8 ozs. sour cream
chopped parsley or chives to
  garnish

Sauté mushrooms and onion in oil for five minutes. Take off heat, add brandy and lemon juice. Chill for several hours stirring occasionally. Toss in sour cream and garnish with parsley or chives.

Rice pilaf from Barbados

2 cups white rice
$\frac{1}{2}$ package lentils
$\frac{1}{2}$ stick butter

1 onion, chopped
salt to taste
thyme to taste

In enough boiling water to cook rice, add lentils and boil for ten minutes. Add chopped onion and butter; add rice and cook according to package directions. Add salt and thyme.
Serve with shrimp curry.

Bridgetown potatoes

3 lbs. potatoes $\frac{1}{2}$ tsp. poultry seasoning
1 onion   salt
1 stick butter   pepper

Boil the potatoes with skin. After potatoes are cooked and cool enough to handle, remove skin and dice. Chop the onion very finely. Melt the butter in a skillet, add the potatoes and onion, and season with the poultry seasoning, salt and pepper to taste. Sauté over very low flame until brown.
Serve with shrimp/scampi.

Dry peas and rice from Barbados

1 lb. dry peas   1 tsp. kitchen bouquet
$\frac{1}{2}$ lb. ham hocks   2 cups Carolina white rice
$\frac{1}{4}$ tsp. thyme   4 cups boiling water

Soak dry peas in 2 cups of water overnight. Remove peas from water and wash thoroughly. Add peas and ham hocks to 4 cups boiling water and cook to soft. Add thyme, kitchen bouquet and white rice. After adding the white rice you can also add more water (a little at a time) if necessary. Cook until rice is tender.
Serve with Brussels sprouts, carrots, cristophene (white squash), roast chicken and white wine.

St Michael's split peas and rice

1 lb. split peas
$2\frac{1}{2}$ cups water
1 large onion chopped
4 slices bacon

$\frac{1}{4}$ tsp. thyme
1 tsp. garlic salt
$\frac{1}{2}$ stick of margarine

Bring water to boil. Add split peas, onion, bacon and thyme and boil for 10 minutes. Add rice, margarine and garlic salt and cook over *low flame* until rice is tender.

Rice à la Pepsi

1 bottle Pepsi-Cola
2 cups water
1 cup rice

$\frac{1}{2}$ cup lentils
$\frac{1}{2}$ onion
$\frac{1}{4}$ lb. fat meat

Sauté onions and fat meat in a frying pan over very low flame. Then add water, Pepsi-Cola and lentils; cook for ten minutes and add salt to taste. Add rice and cook on very low flame.
Serve with Shrimp Creole. Serves 6.

Rice mould

2 cups rice
1 large onion, finely diced
butter or margarine
$\frac{1}{2}$ lb. mushrooms

$\frac{1}{4}$ cup soy sauce
fresh ground pepper
fresh or frozen green peas

Cook rice in lightly salted water and drain. Sauté onion in butter or margarine until tender and lightly browned. Add mushrooms to onion and sauté until tender; combine mushrooms and onion with rice.
Add pepper and soy sauce to taste. Pack in well-greased 10″ or 11″

ring mould. Cover with aluminum foil and bake in moderate oven until piping hot. Unmould and fill centre with cooked fresh or frozen green peas. Serves 8.

Rice pelau from Purchase

1 package Spanish rice (or saffron rice)
1 whole chicken
1 white onion, chopped
4 carrots, cut in cubes

3 stalks celery, cut in cubes
$\frac{1}{4}$ tsp. dry thyme
2 packets beef bouillon
$\frac{1}{3}$ cup raisins
$\frac{1}{4}$ lb. butter

Boil chicken. Remove from broth and let cool. Boil rice, onion, carrots, celery, raisins, spices and butter in chicken broth. (Vegetables should be crisp.) Remove chicken from bones. Add the chicken to the prepared rice. Heat and serve. Serves 6-8.

Soup: Giblet

4 Salads

Barbados Italian salad

2 oz. pasta shells
$\frac{1}{4}$ lb. ham, cooked and sliced
2 oz. black olives, halved and
   stoned

2–3 tblsp. thick mayonnaise
1 tsp. French mustard

Simmer pasta shells in pan of boiling, salted water for about 7 minutes or until just tender. Drain and refresh them.
Shred the ham and mix this with the olives and pasta. Add mustard to mayonnaise and stir enough into salad to bind it together.

St James salt beef salad

12 oz. cooled salt beef, cut into
   Julienne
2 lbs. potatoes (large), boiled in
   jackets
$\frac{1}{2}$ oz. dry mustard

$\frac{1}{2}$ oz. brown sugar
$\frac{1}{4}$ pt. mayonnaise
2 dill pickles, chopped
1 oz. vinegar

Mix mustard, sugar and vinegar. Stir until dissolved. Peel potatoes while hot, slice, layer on to serving dish. Spread with thin coating of mayonnaise, sprinkle on a little of the chopped dill. Cover with a layer of salt beef and moisten with a little of the mustard dressing. Continue until beef and potatoes are used up. Garnish with hard boiled egg and lettuce.

Babb's rice tomato and black olive salad

3 oz. rice	2 oz. black olives
2 ripe tomatoes	3 oz. French dressing
2 oz. button mushrooms	salt and pepper

Boil rice, refresh and drain. Skin tomatoes, remove seeds and cut into eight lengthways. Mix all ingredients leaving some tomato and olives to decorate with. Add French dressing. Decorate and chill.

Babb's kitchen sink salad

(Spring and summer)

chopped celery	dry thyme
chopped red sweet pepper	black pepper
chopped green pepper	mustard (grey puopor)
chopped cauliflower	mayonnaise
black grapes	curry powder
green grapes	raisins
chopped onions	tuna fish
chopped broccoli	chopped parsley

Mix ingredients together and bind with mayonnaise.
Serve with pears.

National breadfruit salad

2 breadfruits	parsley
2 onions	$\frac{1}{2}$ tsp. salt
1 celery bunch	mayonnaise

Peel breadfruit, dice and cook. While cooking add salt. Drain and cool. Chop onions and celery and add to breadfruits with mayonnaise and parsley. Mix well. Serve cold.

Babb's mushroom salad

fresh mushrooms
fresh Boston lettuce, spinach
  and/or chicory

chives
Babb's homemade salad
  dressing

If the mushrooms are small, leave whole; otherwise, halve them. Wash lettuce and mushrooms and let them drain. Cut up some chives and sprinkle over lettuce and mushrooms. Just before serving, pour dressing over salad.

Babb's homemade salad

Salad ingredients:
$\frac{1}{2}$ head lettuce, chopped
$\frac{1}{2}$ head cabbage, chopped
3 stalks celery, chopped
$\frac{1}{2}$ sweet pepper, chopped
4 scallions, chopped
2 English apples, cubed
8 peach halves, sliced
2 carrots, shredded

Dressing ingredients:
$1\frac{1}{2}$ cups mayonnaise
$1\frac{1}{2}$ bottles chilli sauce
1 tbs. horseradish
1 tbs. sugar
1 tsp. Worcestershire sauce
1 tsp. A–1 sauce
$\frac{1}{2}$ tsp. black pepper
1 tsp. mustard
$\frac{1}{2}$ tsp. Tabasco sauce
$\frac{1}{2}$ tsp. thyme

Place the ingredients for the dressing in a bowl and mix thoroughly. Prepare salad ingredients, toss together, and pour dressing over salad.

Tomato Rose salad

Cut tomato in six sections, not quite through to bottom. Fan out to form rose shape.
Serve on crisp lettuce with oil and vinegar dressing.

Egg salad

6 hard-boiled eggs
1 head lettuce
1 green pepper
$\frac{1}{2}$ onion
1 bunch celery

2 carrots
$\frac{1}{2}$ tsp. black pepper
$\frac{1}{2}$ tsp. salt
$\frac{1}{2}$ cup mayonnaise
4 tomatoes

With rough side of grater, shred eggs, lettuce, green pepper, onion, celery and carrots. Place in a large bowl. Season with salt and pepper; mix in mayonnaise.
Place the egg salad on a platter and surround with tomato wedges.
Serve with hot buttered toast for lunch or dinner. Serves 6-8.

Babb's rice tomato and black olive salad

3 ozs. rice
$\frac{1}{4}$ lb. ripe tomatoes
2 ozs. button mushrooms

2 ozs. black olives (stoned)
3 ozs. French dressing
salt and pepper

Boil rice, refresh and drain. Skin tomatoes, remove seeds. Cut into eight lengthways. Mix all ingredients, leaving some tomato and olive to decorate with, add French dressing. Decorate and chill.

Melon salad

1 honeydew or musk melon
  (diced)
1 lb. tomatoes (skinned and
  seeds removed)
$\frac{1}{2}$ lb. cucumber (cut into dice)

salt
1 oz. chopped parsley
1 oz. chopped mint and chives
6 ozs. French dressing

Place diced cucumber and melon in a bowl. Sprinkle with salt. Allow to stand for $\frac{1}{2}$ hour. Drain off any liquid and rinse in cold water. Put melon, cucumber, tomatoes in a bowl, add French dressing. Chill for 2 to 3 hours. Just before serving, add herbs.
N.B. Serve in deep bowl as a lot of juice will be made while the salad is chilling.

Italian salad

$1\frac{1}{2}$ lbs. ham (Julienne)
8 ozs. elbows or shell pasta
8 ozs. mushrooms
4 ozs. black olives (stoned)

Dressing
2 ozs. red wine vinegar
salt and pepper
6 ozs. olive oil
2 ozs. piquant tomato sauce
$\frac{1}{2}$ oz. oregano

Garnish
8 ozs. tomatoes
$\frac{1}{2}$ pint mayonnaise
1 oz. French mustard

Cook and refresh pasta, add mushrooms and olives. Mix dressing, add to pasta, place in serving dish. Garnish.

Babb's combination salad

Salad ingredients:
lettuce
white cabbage
red cabbage
peaches (optional)
apples
celery
tomatoes

Dressing ingredients:
1 bottle chilli sauce
2 tbs. mayonnaise
1 tbs. sugar
1 tbs. horseradish
$\frac{1}{2}$ tbs. thyme
$\frac{1}{2}$ tbs. black pepper
1 tsp. A–1 sauce
1 tsp. Worcestershire sauce

Chop lettuce, red and white cabbage together. Add peaches, apples and celery. Cut tomatoes in wedges. Mix all ingredients together and toss over salad ingredients.

Lettuce and cabbage salad

Mix lettuce with red cabbage, sliced finely, and Italian dressing with thyme, salt and pepper to taste. Serve with tomatoes.

5 Fish

West Indian curried shrimp

3 lbs. shrimp, cooked, shelled,
  de-veined
1 large onion, chopped
2 sweet peppers
$\frac{1}{2}$ stalk celery
$\frac{1}{2}$ cup butter
3 tsp. curry powder

1 bottle chilli sauce
salt to taste
pepper to taste
thyme to taste
dry parsley flakes
1 bottle chutney
Tabasco sauce to taste

In a large pot, sauté onion, celery and peppers in butter for about 20 minutes until tender. Add the rest of the ingredients and the shrimp; cook until thoroughly heated, about 20 minutes.
Serve with lentils and rice. This is better when served the day after it is made and refrigerated.

Serves 6.
Suggested wine: Sauvignon Blanc

Shrimp curry from Freeport

3 lbs. shrimp, shelled, cooked
  and cleaned the day before
$\frac{1}{2}$ stalk celery
1 large onion

salt to taste
1 tsp. thyme
1 tsp. marjoram
1 tbs. Worcestershire sauce

2 sweet peppers
2 cloves garlic
2 sticks butter
1 large can tomato purée
3 tbs. curry powder
1 tbs. A–1 steak sauce

2 tbs. sugar
2 tsp. black pepper
juice of half a lemon
peanuts or slivered almonds
2 tbs. raisins

Chop celery, onion, peppers and garlic and sauté in butter in large frying pan. Remove to large pot or deep casserole and add one large can of tomato purée and simmer until the ingredients are tender. Add curry and drop shrimp into mixture and simmer on very low heat.

Add all other ingredients and cook for about 20–30 minutes until thoroughly blended and well heated.

Suggested wine: Sauvignon Blanc

Mussel salad

(From Babb's kitchen at Pepsi)

1 qt. can of mussels
4 ozs. rice (cooked with mussel liquid)
2 ozs. shallots (finely chopped)
bayleaf (for rice)
1 head celery, cut into one inch sticks

4 ozs. button mushrooms, sliced
juice of $\frac{1}{2}$ lemon
fresh ground pepper
4 ozs. double cream
1 oz. chopped parsley
$\frac{1}{4}$ pint chicken stock

Drain mussels. Reserve liquid for cooking rice. Put oil into saucepan, add chopped shallots and rice. Make up mussel liquid to $\frac{1}{2}$ pint with chicken stock. Add to rice with bayleaf. Cover and cook for 18 minutes. Turn out and allow to cool. Put mussels and mushrooms in the lemon juice and pepper. Allow to marinate. When rice is quite cold, mix celery, mussels, mushroom into rice. Taste for seasoning, then add cream.

Serve sprinkled with the chopped parsley.

Shrimp salad

$2\frac{1}{2}$ lbs. fresh shrimp
1 whole head lettuce
1 green pepper
4 scallions
$\frac{1}{2}$ onion
3 stalks celery
1 raw carrot, peeled and
   shredded
4 radishes
2 fresh apples

2 large tomatoes
1 small cucumber
1 lemon
$\frac{1}{2}$ tsp. black pepper
$\frac{1}{2}$ tsp. poultry seasoning
$\frac{1}{2}$ tsp. thyme
$\frac{1}{2}$ tsp. salt
$\frac{1}{2}$ cup Wish Bone salad dressing

Boil shrimp with $\frac{1}{2}$ teaspoon salt and one whole lemon cut in half, for 25 minutes. Let cool then clean.
Chop lettuce, pepper, scallions, onion, celery, radishes, apples, tomatoes and cucumber. Cut shrimp in half and discard tail ends. Mix all ingredients together and season with pepper, poultry seasoning and thyme. Add salad dressing and toss. Serves 6.

Babb's special fish from Barbados

4 lbs. fish steaks
juice of $\frac{1}{2}$ lemon
1 large onion, sliced very thin
   (into rings)
2 fresh tomatoes, sliced
$\frac{1}{2}$ tsp. salt
$\frac{1}{2}$ tsp. black pepper

$\frac{1}{2}$ tsp. thyme
3 cloves garlic, finely chopped
1 can tomato paste
1 cup water
1 tsp. mustard
butter

Place fish in bowl with lemon juice and salt over it. Let stand for 30 minutes and then rinse off. Cover bottom of baking pan with half the onion slices and place fish on top. Sprinkle fish with mixture of salt, black pepper, and thyme. Cover fish with remainder of onion slices and sliced tomatoes. Sprinkle with garlic.
Mix tomato paste with one cup water and mustard. Pour over fish and dot butter on top. Bake in oven at 350°F, covered, for 45 minutes.

Remove cover and continue baking for another 20 minutes. Serves 8-10.
Serve with mashed potatoes or Rice à la Pepsi

Suggested wine: Weber Moselblumchen

Clams oregano

2 dozen clams in shells, well-
  scrubbed
$\frac{3}{4}$ cup melted butter or
  margarine
1 cup packaged dry
  breadcrumbs

2 cloves garlic, crushed
2 tbs. chopped parsley
2 tbs. grated Parmesan cheese
4 tsp. lemon juice
1 tsp. dried oregano leaves
$\frac{1}{8}$ tsp. liquid hot pepper

In large flat pan, bring $\frac{1}{2}$ inch water to boil. Add clams and simmer, covered, until clams open, 6 to 10 minutes. Meanwhile, in a medium-size bowl, combine butter with breadcrumbs, garlic, chopped parsley, Parmesan cheese, lemon juice, oregano, and hot pepper.
Remove the clams from pan; discard top shells. Remove clams from bottom shells; chop coarsely, and add to crumb mixture. Spoon into bottom shells.
Arrange filled clam shells in large roasting pan and sprinkle with water to dampen. Run under broiler just until golden-brown for about 5 minutes. Garnish with lemon wedges and parsley sprigs. Serve at once. Serves 8.

Babb's homemade salmon from Pepsi Kitchen

8 fresh salmon steaks
salt
pepper

$\frac{1}{2}$ cup butter
1 tsp. mustard
$\frac{1}{2}$ tsp. black pepper

1 onion
$\frac{2}{3}$ cup white wine
$\frac{1}{3}$ cup flour
1 cup milk
$\frac{1}{4}$ lb. grated cheese, any kind

1 tsp. lemon juice
$\frac{1}{2}$ tsp chicken poultry seasoning
lemons
watercress

Place salmon steaks in large skillet and add enough water to cover. Season with salt and pepper and add several slices of onion. Simmer for one hour. When water gets low, add $\frac{2}{3}$ cup wine. When cooked, take salmon out of water and let it cool to room temperature.

Meanwhile, prepare sauce. Melt butter, stir in flour, slowly add milk; then add grated cheese and stir until melted. Cook sauce over low flame as these ingredients are added. Season with mustard, black pepper, lemon juice and chicken poultry seasoning.

Halve several lemons. Place salmon on platter, surround with halved lemons and watercress. Pour sauce on top or serve in gravy boat. Serves 8.

Serve with tiny white boiled potatoes covered with melted butter and minced parsley and boiled fresh asparagus covered with a mixture of melted butter and lemon juice.

Dessert: Fresh strawberries sprinkled with sugar and topped with cream followed by coffee.

Wine suggestion: Puligny-Montrachet (a Monsieur Henri selection), 1970.

Fish pie from Bagshot House

3 lbs. fish steaks (halibut,
    swordfish or any other)
lemon juice
salt
pepper
thyme
3 tomatoes

$\frac{1}{2}$ large onion
1 tsp. mustard
carrots
cauliflower
potatoes, sliced
1 tbs. chilli sauce
$\frac{1}{2}$ cup butter

Place fish in pan and sprinkle salt and lemon juice on both sides. Let it stand about $\frac{1}{2}$ hour. Rinse. Place butter in frying pan; add sliced tomatoes, onions, fish, water, salt, pepper and thyme. Add chilli

sauce, mustard, and cook slowly until tender.

Boil fresh carrots, cauliflower and sliced potatoes for about 20 minutes with salt to taste. Drain.

In baking dish, arrange a layer of vegetables and a layer of fish, previously cut into chunks. Leave overnight in refrigerator. When ready to serve the next day, put pie in oven at 300°F until warmed through.

Suggested wine: Weber Moselblumchen

Babb's fish fillets from Freeport

3–6 lbs. fish fillets (any kind)	pepper to taste
1½ lemons	thyme to taste
½ cup milk	butter
1 egg	paprika
salt to taste	

Place fish in a pan and squeeze lemons over fish. Sprinkle salt over the fillets and let them stand for approximately 25 minutes. Remove fish from pan and rinse off salt and lemon juice. Place the fillets back into a greased baking pan. Sprinkle salt, pepper, and thyme over fish. Beat milk and egg together and pour this mixture over fillets. Place a few pats of butter on top of the fish and sprinkle paprika over it. Bake at 300°F for approximately 1 hour (or until cooked).

Suggested wine: Sauvignon Blanc

Shrimp creole from Nassau

3 lbs. raw shrimp	½ tsp. black pepper
1 large onion, coarsely chopped	¼ tsp. thyme
1 large green sweet pepper, coarsely chopped	dash of garlic
	2 small cans stewed tomatoes
4 celery stalks, chopped	1 stick butter or margarine

Melt butter in frying pan over low heat. Add shrimp and remaining ingredients. Cover and gently steam until vegetables are tender and shrimp is cooked. Serve over white rice. Serves 6–8.

Crabmeat salad

2 lbs. frozen crabmeat
4 stalks celery, diced
1 green pepper, chopped very fine
1 onion, chopped very fine
1 tsp. horseradish
1 tsp. Hollandaise sauce
1 tsp. prepared mustard
$\frac{1}{4}$ tsp. Tabasco sauce
1 cup mayonnaise

$\frac{1}{2}$ tsp. black pepper
$\frac{1}{2}$ tsp. thyme
$\frac{1}{4}$ tsp. poultry seasoning
4 pears (canned), chopped
2 fresh apples, chopped
4 tomatoes, cut in wedges
6 radishes, cut in rose design
scallions
lettuce
parsley

Place defrosted crabmeat in a large bowl. Add all ingredients, except for the tomatoes, parsley, radishes, lettuce, and scallions. Mix well. Place lettuce on serving platter and arrange crabmeat salad over lettuce. Garnish salad with tomatoes, parsley, radishes, and scallions. This salad can also be stuffed into tomatoes.

Suggested wine: Puligny-Montrachet, 1970

Tuna salad from Purchase

2 lbs. white tuna in water (drained)
4 stalks celery, diced
1 green pepper, chopped very fine
1 onion, chopped very fine
1 tsp. horseradish
1 tsp. Hollandaise sauce
1 tsp. prepared mustard
1 tsp. Tabasco sauce

1 cup mayonnaise
$\frac{1}{2}$ tsp. black pepper
$\frac{1}{2}$ tsp. thyme
$\frac{1}{4}$ tsp. poultry seasoning
4 peaches (canned), chopped
lettuce
4 tomatoes, cut in wedges
parsley
6 radishes
scallions

Place tuna in a large bowl, add mayonnaise and all other ingredients, except tomatoes, parsley, radishes, lettuce and scallions. Mix well. Place lettuce around serving platter and arrange tuna over lettuce. Garnish salad with tomatoes, parsley, radishes and scallions. This salad can also be served stuffed into tomatoes.

Suggested wine: Weber Moselblumchen, 1972

Babb's famous salmon from Pepsi

8 fresh salmon steaks
salt
pepper
1 onion

Garnish
sliced lemon
watercress

Wine sauce
4 tbs. butter
4 tbs. flour
$1\frac{1}{3}$ cup milk
$\frac{2}{3}$ cup white wine
$\frac{1}{4}$ lb. grated Swiss or Cheddar
  cheese
1 tsp. prepared mustard
$\frac{1}{2}$ tsp. black pepper
$\frac{1}{2}$ tsp. poultry seasoning
1 tsp. lemon juice

Season salmon with salt and pepper. Place in large skillet with sliced onion and add water to cover. Simmer for one hour or until cooked. Remove from water and cool at room temperature. Prepare sauce while salmon is cooling.

In a medium-size saucepan, using low heat, melt butter. Add flour and stir constantly until a smooth paste is formed. Continue stirring and add milk, wine and grated cheese. When sauce begins to thicken, add mustard, pepper, poultry seasoning and lemon juice. Stir until sauce begins to bubble gently.

Place salmon on platter. Spoon sauce over each steak. Garnish with sliced lemon and watercress.

Serve with fresh asparagus and tiny boiled parsley potatoes.

Dessert: Fresh strawberries topped with sweetened whipped cream.
Wine: Puligny-Montrachet 1970 (a Monsieur Henri Selection)

West Indian style shrimp/scampi

3 lbs. fresh shrimp/scampi
$\frac{1}{2}$ fresh lemon
$\frac{1}{2}$ tsp. black pepper
$\frac{1}{4}$ tsp. garlic powder
$\frac{1}{2}$ tsp. Tabasco sauce

$\frac{1}{2}$ tsp. poultry seasoning
$\frac{1}{2}$ tsp. thyme
$\frac{1}{2}$ tsp. curry powder
2 sticks butter
flour

Cook the shrimp in boiling salted water with the lemon half. After the shrimp is cooked and cool enough to handle, shell and de-vein. Mix together the pepper, garlic powder, Tabasco sauce, poultry seasoning, thyme and curry powder. Marinate the shrimp in this mixture for approximately 25 minutes.

Melt the butter in a skillet. Dip the shrimp in the flour and fry until golden brown. Serve with Bridgetown potatoes. Serves 4–6.

Suggested wine: Sauvignon Blanc

Fillet of dolphin with grapefruit and Hollandaise sauce

6 portions of dolphin
1 pint court bouillon
1 pint Hollandaise sauce

2 large grapefruit cut into segments

Prepare dolphin and poach in bouillon until tender. Heat grapefruit segments. Place two or three segments on each portion of fish. Serve Hollandaise sauce separately.

Flaked fish with tomato concasse

Flavour some mayonnaise with garlic and a little tomato paste. Place tomato concasse in a scallop shell, add flaked seasoned fish, mask with sauce, garnish with red pimento and parsley.

St Lawrence devilled kingfish/dolphin

10 kingfish steaks
5 oz. butter
4 tsp. curry powder
2 tsp. Worcestershire sauce

3 tblsp. sultanas
2 tblsp. chutney
6 tblsp. soft breadcrumbs
salt and pepper to taste

Melt butter, blend in curry powder, add Worcestershire sauce, sultanas, chutney, salt and pepper. Add breadcrumbs. Spread mixture over the top of the fish and bake at 400°F. Garnish with lime and parsley. Serves 10.

Ceviche

5 lbs. raw fish, skinless and
    bone free
3 minced onions
1 oz. olive oil

2 cups lime juice
yellow hot pepper, minced

Cut fish into cubes, place in glass dish. Cover with rest of ingredients. Stir. Store in refrigerator for 2 days. Serve on bed of lettuce. Garnish with cucumber, tomato and parsley.

Christchurch tuna fish salad

.4 tins tuna fish, flaked
4 apples, diced
8 cooked potatoes, diced
8 sticks celery, diced
8 oz. peas
1 lb. cooked beetroot, diced
$\frac{1}{2}$ lb. tomatoes
2 oz. parsley

Dressing:
12 oz. mayonnaise
8 oz. plain yogurt
salt and pepper
castor sugar
1 clove garlic, crushed

Place flaked tuna, potatoes and apple in a bowl. Add dressing. Turn out onto serving dish. Add celery, beetroot and peas. Garnish with· tomatoes and parsley.

St Lucy crab and rice salad

1 lb. crabmeat
12 oz. rice (cook and refresh)
1 green sweet pepper (blanch
    and cut into julienne)
salt and pepper
1 clove garlic
6 oz. black olives, stoned
4 oz. mushrooms, sliced
2 oz. walnuts, coarsley chopped

Dressing
juice of 2 lemons
4 oz. olive oil
salt and pepper, freshly milled

Combine ingredients for dressing. Season rice and dressing then add sweet pepper, olives, mushrooms and crabmeat. Dress on serving dish. Sprinkle with walnuts.

Shrimp Bob

$\frac{1}{2}$ oz. oil (peanut)
1 hot pepper, seeded and
    chopped
2 oz. peanut butter
1 small onion chopped

salt and black pepper
8 shrimps
1 tsp. sugar
1 oz. water
radishes for garnish

In a skillet heat oil, add hot pepper, peanut butter, onion, salt and black pepper. Add shrimps, sugar and water. Cook until shrimps are just cooked. Serve cold on bed of lettuce. Garnish with parsley and radishes.

St Lawrence devilled kingfish/dolphin

10 kingfish steaks
5 oz. butter
4 tsp. curry powder
2 tsp. Worcestershire sauce
3 tblsp. sultanas

1 tblsp. chutney
6 tblsp. soft breadcrumbs
salt and pepper
slices of lime and chopped
    parsley for garnish

Melt butter, blend in curry powder, add Worcestershire sauce, sultanas and chutney, salt and pepper, add bread crumbs. Spread mixture over the top of the fish and bake at 400°F. Garnish with lime and parsley.

Spring salmon luncheon

Rinse salmon and place in large poaching pan. Cover with water and add:

Half a seasoning packet from
    Uncle Ben's Long Grain
    Wild Rice Blend
$\frac{1}{2}$ dstsp. garlic powder

$\frac{1}{2}$ dstsp. garlic salt
4 cubes chicken bouillon
3 lemons, cut up
$\frac{1}{4}$ tsp. black pepper

Steam for $\frac{1}{2}$ hour. Take salmon out of pan, let stand for 10 minutes and take skin off (while still hot).
Serve with a salad made from the following and dressed with blue cheese.

water cress
cucumber
mushrooms
bibb lettuce
sweet peppers

red onions
parsley
fresh strawberries
celery

Beverage: iced tea

Fishcakes from Babb's Executive Kitchen

1 large can tuna
4 sticks celery
3 large onions
3 red sweet peppers

1 tsp. dry thyme
1 tsp. black pepper
2 tblsp. A–1 sauce
$\frac{1}{2}$ tsp. Tabasco sauce

Mix above ingredients in blender and pour into large bowl. Then add:

2 cups flour
1 cup half and half

1 dstsp. baking powder
3 tblsp. chopped parsley

Mix thoroughly and deep fry. Fishcakes should be the size of a medium spoon, round shape.

Babb's dolphin and kingfish from Speightstown

3 or 4 lbs. fish
1 lime
$\frac{1}{2}$ tsp. salt
4 eggs
$\frac{1}{4}$ tsp. dry thyme

$\frac{1}{2}$ cup flour
$\frac{1}{2}$ cup breadcrumbs
$\frac{1}{4}$ tsp. black pepper
1 tblsp. cooking oil

Cut fish into steaks, squeeze lime on fish portions. Add salt and set aside for 20 minutes. Beat eggs, add thyme and set aside. Mix flour and breadcrumbs and set aside.
Wash fish thoroughly, add salt and black pepper. Dip fish portions in egg mix first, then in flour mix. Fry until golden crisp over a very slow fire.
Serve with string beans and yam pie.

Soup: Manhattan Clam Chowder

Babb's codfish Barbados

2 lbs. boneless salt cod
2 lbs. fresh okra (cooked for 15
   minutes) *or* 2 pkgs. frozen
   okra
3 tomatoes, large, chopped

1 onion, large, chopped
1 stick butter
$\frac{1}{4}$ tsp. thyme
$\frac{1}{4}$ tsp. black pepper

Boil cod in lots of water for 1 hr. Drain. Boil a second time for $\frac{1}{2}$ hr. and drain.

Chop the cod, and place in a frying pan in the melted butter. Add okra and all remaining ingredients. Simmer 45 minutes, covered. Serves 4–6.

Serve with plain rice, tossed salad and iced tea or Pepsi-Cola.

Crane Beach flying fish

6 flying fish
1 lime
1 lemon
$\frac{3}{4}$ tsp. salt
2 onions
$\frac{1}{2}$ tsp. fresh thyme
$\frac{1}{2}$ tsp. cloves, ground

2 pegs fresh garlic
$\frac{1}{4}$ tsp. lime juice
$\frac{1}{2}$ hot pepper
3 tomatoes
1 stick butter
$\frac{1}{4}$ tsp. black pepper

Place flying fish in bowl, squeeze over lime, add $\frac{1}{2}$ teaspoon of salt and let it sit for 25 minutes.

Prepare seasoning: chop onion, fresh garlic and hot pepper. Add fresh thyme, cloves, $\frac{1}{4}$ tsp. salt and lime juice.

Wash fish thoroughly, place in bowl and sprinkle with black pepper and $\frac{1}{4}$ tsp. salt. Spread prepared seasoning through inside of fish.

In frying pan, melt margarine, place 1 layer of onion slices in pan, then the fish covered with onion and tomato slices. Steam for approximately 45 minutes.

Serve with the coocoo and Banks beer.

Soup: Seafood Gumbo

Babb's codfish Creole

4 slices codfish
3 tomatoes
2 large onions
1 envelope chicken concentrate
  (powdered)

1 tblsp. butter
2 tblsp. breadcrumbs
salt and pepper to taste

Plunge tomatoes into boiling water for a few seconds and then into cold water and peel. Cut into slices. Cut onions into slices.

Butter baking dish, place onions and tomato slices in baking dish and top with slices of codfish. Salt and pepper lightly.

Dissolve chicken concentrate in 1 cup of boiling water, add to the fish. Sprinkle breadcrumbs and dot with butter.

Bake at 350°F for 30 minutes. Baste during cooking. Serves 4.

Fishcakes from Brooklyn

West Indian dish

Boil 2 lbs. cod fish for $\frac{1}{2}$ hour. Strain off and boil again for $\frac{1}{2}$ hour. Mix together:

2 cups flour
6 eggs
$\frac{1}{4}$ tsp. dried thyme
$\frac{1}{2}$ tsp. black pepper
$\frac{1}{2}$ tsp. Tabasco

2 tsp. baking powder
Chop and mix 1 head parsley
  into ingredients
$\frac{1}{2}$ tsp. garlic salt and powder

Pour cooking oil into frying pan and heat. Chop cod fish in mixing bowl. Add other ingredients and mix. When cooking oil is hot, take one tsp. at a time of mixture and place into hot oil very slowly. Fry until brown.

Can be taken on excursions; excellent with cocktails and summer dishes, à la Babb.

Coocoo from Barbados
(served with flying fish)

1 lb. meal   3 pints water
$\frac{1}{2}-\frac{3}{4}$ lb. okra, sliced $\frac{1}{2}$ oz. salt

Boil okra in 2 pints water for 45 minutes, then remove from heat and pour entire contents into bowl. Put meal, 1 pint cold water and salt into a saucepan and cook over low heat for 25 minutes, stirring constantly.

Next, drain water from okra at five-minute intervals, adding it to the meal; at the same time, gradually add some of the meal to the okra. This process should continue for 30–45 minutes, depending on the consistency desired.

Serve with any meat or fish.

Gougons marinade

Slice 1 carrot, 1 onion and sauté in $\frac{1}{2}$ cup oil with five cloves garlic. Add 1 cup vinegar, $\frac{1}{2}$ cup water salt and pepper, little thyme and bay leaf and 1 chopped pimento. Bring liquid to boil and simmer for 15 minutes. Pour over fish gougons and marinate for 24 hours.

6 Meat and Poultry

Prime ribs from Dalton Manor

Place foil in bottom of pan. Rub $\frac{1}{2}$ tsp. of dry thyme, $\frac{1}{2}$ tsp. black pepper, $\frac{1}{2}$ tsp. garlic salt and powder and 1 whole onion on meat. Put in 1 stick of butter and 1 tbls. A–1 Sauce and 1 tsp. of Worcestershire sauce. Cover with foil for 1 hour at 400°F, then baste til brown.

Soup: Vegetable Soup

Prime ribs from Bagshot House

Sprinkle prime ribs with garlic salt, dry thyme and black pepper. Place meat in casserole with a stick of butter.
Place in oven at 350°F and bake for 1 hour. Baste meat with juices to brown.
Serve with baked potato wrapped in aluminum foil (choice of butter or sour cream with potato), broccoli and a tossed green salad.

Soup: French Onion
Desert: Fresh Fruit Salad
Beverage: White wine

Babb's supreme shepherd's pie

1 large can tomato purée
6 lbs. of chopped meat
3 large onions (chopped)
3 sweet green/peppers
  (chopped)
1 head of celery (chopped)
$\frac{1}{2}$ tsp. dry thyme

$\frac{1}{2}$ tsp. black pepper
$\frac{1}{2}$ tsp. garlic salt
4 pkgs. of beef boullion
1 bottle of A–1 sauce
2 tbsps. of Worcestershire
  sauce
$\frac{1}{2}$ tsp. Tabasco sauce

Put all the ingredients in a large frying pan and cook for 45 minutes.
Cook and mash 12 potatoes with 2 sticks of butter. ·
Cook 1 large box of frozen carrots and 1 large box of frozen peas
together for ten minutes.
Place layer of meat in large casserole, then layer of carrots and peas.
Place mashed potatoes on top for covering. Place in oven at 300°F for
20 minutes. Take casserole out of oven and place grated American
cheese on top, place casserole back in oven to brown.
Serve with bottle of white wine and tossed green salad.

Soup: Oxtail

Beefsteak from St Lawrence

6 lbs. chopped beef
2 onions chopped
2 sweet peppers, chopped
4 stalks of celery
$\frac{1}{2}$ tsp. garlic salt
$\frac{1}{2}$ tsp. garlic powder
$\frac{1}{2}$ tsp. dried thyme

$\frac{1}{2}$ tsp. black pepper
1 tsp. A–1 Sauce
1 tsp. Worcestershire sauce
1 bottle ketchup
1 lb. fresh mushrooms,
  chopped

Mix all ingredients together and form into patties. Dip patties into
flour and fry gently until brown.
Serve with French fries and a tossed salad

Soup: French Onion

Babb's sirloin roast dinner from Nassau

Appetizer suggestion: Wine consommé, prepared with one part red wine to three parts beef consommé

Serve the slices of the sirloin roast with:
French-style green beans and almonds
Creamed onions, prepared with tiny white pearl onions and cream sauce
Baked potato, served with sour cream and chives

Salad suggestion: Tossed salad, prepared with tomato, lettuce, cucumber and green pepper
Dessert suggestion: Strawberries and port; fresh strawberries sprinkled with sugar and Hooper's port of 1937 poured over them
Wine suggestion: Beaujolais St Andre, 1971

Babb's island pot roast

6 to 8 lbs. beef	1 tblsp. Worcestershire sauce
salt and pepper	1 jigger sherry
dry thyme	3 beef bouillon cubes
bay leaf	1 chopped onion
1 stick of butter	3 tomatoes
1 can tomato paste	3 sticks celery
2 tblsp. A–1 sauce	1 green pepper

Sprinkle salt and pepper on meat, mix dry thyme and bay leaf and sprinkle generously over beef. Place in casserole dish, and pour Babb's special ingredients over meat. Cover and bake at 350°F for 30 minutes, take cover off and baste and let brown for another 30 minutes. Meat must be cooked until tender, not well done! Serve with noodles and baby carrots

Soup: French Onion
Dessert: Ice cream with chocolate sauce
Beverage: Red wine, coffee, night cap of brandy

Dalton's corned beef casserole

6 lbs corned beef
1 large onion
3 red peppers
6 stalks celery
8 potatoes, peeled and cooked

$\frac{1}{2}$ tsp. thyme
$\frac{1}{2}$ tsp. garlic salt and powder
$\frac{1}{4}$ tsp. black pepper
4 eggs
6 pkgs. of beef broth

Mix ingredients in blender. Place in bowl and hand mix again. Grease casserole dish with butter. Place ingredients in casserole dish. Preheat oven to 350°F. Bake approximately $\frac{1}{2}$ hour. Before serving, sprinkle cheese on top. Serve when cheese is brown.
Serve with peas and corn or rice.

Marinated sliced beef

1 lb. cooked beef (Julienne)
1 onion, sliced
salt and pepper

$\frac{1}{2}$ oz. lemon juice
1 cup sour cream

Sprinkle lemon juice on beef, add onion, salt and pepper and sour cream. Mix. Serve on leaf of lettuce. Garnish.

Tarragon paté

Sauté in a pan

$\frac{1}{4}$ cup butter
$\frac{1}{3}$ cup minced seasoning

$1\frac{1}{2}$ tbs. chopped tarragon
1 lb. chicken livers

Blend 2 eggs with 3 ozs. fresh cream combine with liver puree, salt and pepper. Bake in usual way. Chill.

Brisket of beef à la Antigua

1–4 lbs. first cut brisket of beef
3–4 large onions
2 cans Campbell's tomato soup
1 bottle Heinz catsup (medium size)

salt
freshly ground pepper
garlic powder

Into a large roasting pan (with high sides) slice onions to cover pan. Cover the onions with catsup. Place brisket on top of onions and catsup. Season brisket with salt, pepper and garlic powder. Cover brisket with tomato soup (undiluted). Bring up from bottom, some of the onion and catsup mixture. Cover pan tightly with aluminum foil and bake at 300°F for about 3–4 hours until tender. There should be gravy almost to the top of the pan. Slice thinly.
This tastes better if it is made the day before, sliced, returned to gravy and refrigerated to marinate. Serve over noodles. Serves 6–8.

Dessert suggestion: Apple pie à la mode
Suggested wine: Chateau Gaillard de la Gorce, 1967

Corned beef hash from St Vincent

$\frac{1}{4}$ cup butter ($\frac{1}{2}$ stick)
1 onion, chopped
2 sticks celery hearts, chopped
6 potatoes, boiled
3 medium-sized cans of corned beef
$\frac{1}{2}$ tsp. thyme
$\frac{1}{2}$ tsp. black pepper

Potatoes
$\frac{1}{2}$ cup butter (1 stick)
1 onion, chopped finely
2 lbs. boiled potatoes, cubed
1 tsp. salt

Melt butter in skillet; add chopped onion and celery to sauté. Meanwhile, mash the boiled potatoes. Mix in corned beef with potato. When onion and celery are golden, add to corned beef. Then add seasonings and mix thoroughly.
Form into 6 to 8 patties. Broil patties 15 minutes on each side. Serves 6–8.

Melt butter in skillet for browning potatoes. When they just begin to turn golden, add chopped onion. Season with salt.

Salad suggestion: Tomato and lettuce salad with Seven Seas salad dressing.
Dessert suggestion: Fresh fruit salad

Montrose Village meatloaf

2 lbs. ground sirloin steak
2 small cans stewed
   tomatoes

4 slices cracked wheat
   bread (crusts removed)
$\frac{3}{4}$ of a package onion soup
   mix

Mix all ingredients together. Form into the shape of a loaf and bake for one hour at 350°F. Serves 6–8.

St Lawrence goulash

3 lbs. round steak
2 tbs. butter
1 tbs. kitchen bouquet
$\frac{1}{2}$ onion, finely chopped
6 stalks celery
3 medium carrots
1 package frozen peas
water

1 tbs. chilli sauce
1 tsp. A–1 sauce
1 tsp. Worcestershire sauce
1 tsp. dry thyme
2 onions, cut in quarters
salt
black pepper

Cut round steak into 1-inch pieces, sprinkle with salt and black pepper and $\frac{1}{2}$ tsp. dry thyme. Place in bowl and set aside for 30 minutes.
Melt butter in frying pan, add meat, kitchen bouquet, chopped onion, green pepper, three stalks celery (finely chopped). Cover and

simmer over low heat, stirring occasionally, for one hour or until meat is tender.

Add ½ teaspoon dry thyme, ½ teaspoon black pepper, gradually stir in one cup water. Add chilli sauce, A–1 sauce and Worcestershire sauce. Taste for flavour. Refrigerate overnight.

Remove from refrigerator ½ hour before serving. Add ½ cup water, return to stove and simmer over low heat until thoroughly hot. While meat is simmering, cut carrots and remaining celery in 1–inch slices, onions in quarters. Place in two cups salted water and cook over low heat for ½ hour; drain off water. (Quartered potatoes may also be added.) Cook peas according to package directions.

Just before serving, mix meat and vegetables and serve on heated plates. Optional serving: place vegetables on plate, serve meat and gravy on top. Serves 6.

Suggested wine: Yago Condal

Chopped steak St Thomas

2 lbs. ground round or sirloin
    steak (lean)
1 onion chopped
3 stalks celery, chopped

1 tsp. thyme
salt to taste
pepper to taste
3 tbs. butter

Sauté onion, celery, salt and pepper in butter. Spread out hamburger meat on cutting board; put onion and celery mixture in centre; mix thoroughly, form into thick patties; broil in pre-heated broiler until done. Serves 4–6.

Note: You may add crumbled bacon to above mixture for variety.

Steak tartare à la Babb

6 slices pumpernickel bread
    (crusts removed)
1 lb. lean ground beef

Tabasco or red pepper sauce to
    taste
salt to taste

$\frac{1}{2}$ medium onion, very finely
   chopped
1 egg yolk
Worcestershire sauce

black pepper to taste
dry mustard to taste
lemon juice to taste

Mix beef with egg yolks and onion and season with above seasonings.
Serve open faced on pumpernickel. Garnish with parsley.
Serve for lunch with cold beer.

St Croix goulash

3 lbs. sirloin steak, cubed
1 large onion, chopped
3 stalks celery, chopped
1 large tomato, cut in small
   wedges
$\frac{1}{2}$ cup butter
$\frac{1}{2}$ cup water
salt

pepper
$\frac{1}{2}$ tsp. black pepper
$\frac{1}{2}$ tsp. celery salt
$\frac{1}{2}$ tsp. thyme
$\frac{1}{2}$ tsp. poultry seasoning
$\frac{1}{2}$ tsp. garlic salt
1 tbs. kitchen bouquet

In butter in a large skillet, brown steak cubes for about 25 minutes.
After meat is well-browned, add the onion, celery and tomatoes,
along with other ingredients and water. Simmer for an additional
$1\frac{1}{2}$ hours, covered. Serves 6.
Serve with noodles and fresh asparagus tips with Hollandaise sauce.
For dessert, serve vanilla ice cream smothered in chopped pineapple.

Suggested wine: Yago Condal

Leg of lamb from St James

leg of lamb
2 stalks celery
2 large onions
12 potatoes, peeled
$\frac{1}{2}$ cup sherry

$\frac{1}{2}$ tsp. celery salt
$\frac{1}{2}$ tsp. thyme
$\frac{1}{2}$ tsp. poultry seasoning
$\frac{1}{2}$ tsp. black pepper
$\frac{1}{2}$ tsp. salt

Chop, very small, one onion and celery and set aside. Mix sherry and other ingredients (celery salt, thyme, poultry seasoning, pepper and salt) well. Bore holes in lamb and stuff with celery and onion mixture and baste sherry mixture over lamb and into dressing holes.

Slice another onion into rings, and place around lamb in baking pan and cook at 350°F for about 3 hours.

About $\frac{1}{2}$ hour before lamb is done, place potatoes around lamb and baste with drippings. Serve with fresh cauliflower with cream sauce. Serves 8–10.

Dessert suggestion: Hot apple pie with vanilla ice cream
Wine suggestion: Piat en Pot

Broiled boned leg of lamb

1 leg of lamb, boned and split
   lengthwise

$\frac{1}{3}$ bottle of Milani 1890 Dressing
   (for each half of lamb)

Marinate for four to five hours, turning frequently. Broil for ten minutes on each side. Slice lamb at an angle. Serves 4 (each half)

Suggested wine: Chateau La Libarde

Broiled lamb chops

12 lamb chops (2 per person)
salt to taste

pepper to taste
thyme to taste

Sprinkle chops with salt, pepper and thyme on both sides. Let stand for one hour.

Approximately 25 minutes before serving, place chops under broiler at position closest to heat. Turn over chops once while broiling.

Serve with string beans or peas, almonds and mushrooms, and baked potato. Serves 6.

Appetizer suggestion: Cottage cheese salad, prepared with lettuce, cottage cheese, two wedges of tomato, two peach halves *or* creamy mushroom soup, prepared with one can of mushroom soup and one can of half and half.

Dessert suggestion: Apple pie à la mode, served with cherry on top *or* vanilla ice cream.

Wine suggestion: Red Burgundy, preferably Nuits Saint Georges, 1969

Babb's favourite Irish stew

6 lb. lamb kabobs
juice of 1 lemon
salt
$\frac{1}{4}$ tsp. dried thyme
$\frac{1}{4}$ tsp. black pepper
$\frac{1}{2}$ tsp. garlic salt
1 tsp. Worcestershire sauce
1 tsp. A-1 sauce
1 stick margarine
1 chopped onion
3 chopped tomatoes

1 can cream of mushroom
   soup
1 tbsp. flour
2 tbsp. milk
1 head cauliflower
2 lb. carrots, cut up
1 bunch celery, chopped
2 lb. small white potatoes
2 lb. small white onions
1 large box frozen peas

Soak salted lamb kabobs in lemon juice for 20 minutes, then rinse. Combine seasonings; thyme, pepper, garlic salt, Worcestershire sauce and A-1 sauce with lamb. Melt margarine in skillet. Add chopped onion, chopped tomatoes and lamb. Cook over very slow fire for 45 minutes.

While lamb is cooking, cook the cauliflower, carrots, and celery in 2 cups boiling salted water for 20 minutes. Peel onions and boil for 15 minutes. Boil potatoes for 20 minutes. Drain vegetables.

When lamb has cooked for 45 minutes, add cream of mushroom soup and flour mixed with milk. Cook for an additional 15 minutes. In a casserole dish, put down a layer of lamb, then a layer of vegetables, and so forth until ingredients are used up. Sprinkle peas on top. Cover casserole and put in oven at 300°F for 25 minutes before serving. Serve with a lettuce and tomato salad with oil and vinegar dressing.

Soup: Cream of Corn

Grilled lamb chops

Place lamb chops in a casserole and sprinkle with dry thyme, black pepper and garlic salt on one side. Grill to brown then turn over and repeat on second side
Serve with baby potatoes, baby carrots (both garnished with chopped parsley), peas and a tossed green spinach salad.

Soup: Oxtail
Dessert: Apple pie
Beverages: White wine, coffee

Babb's holiday leg of pork

4 lb. leg of pork	1 tsp. dry thyme
1 tsp. salt	3 garlic pegs
1 tsp. black pepper	2 small onions
1 sweet pepper	$\frac{1}{4}$ lb. butter
3 sticks celery	lemon

Place leg of pork in baking pan. Rub with lemon and salt, and let stand for approximately $\frac{1}{2}$ hour.
Chop up sweet pepper, 1 onion, celery, dry thyme, black pepper, salt, garlic. Place finely chopped ingredients on board.
Rinse pork and sprinkle with salt and pepper. With kitchen knife, bore holes in the pork and stuff with chopped ingredients. Place in baking pan. Place sliced onion on top of pork. Also place butter (in chunks) on top of pork. Bake at 300°F for approximately 2 hours.

Potatoes
Peel potatoes and place against pork approximately $\frac{1}{2}$ hour before pork is done. Baste with juice from pork and turn gradually.

String beans
Steam, add a few almonds.

Salad suggestion: Lettuce and tomato tossed.
Dessert suggestion: Fresh fruit salad.
Wine suggestion: Puligny-Montrachet, 1970, Clos du Chaniot (a Monsieur Henri Selection)

A way with sausage

2 lbs. sausage (any type)   salt
1 sweet pepper   pepper
1 large onion   celery
butter

Steam sausages by placing in pan with small amount of water and simmering for about $\frac{1}{2}$ hour with closed cover. Sauté in butter, the sliced onion, pepper and diced celery, with salt and pepper.
Serve onion mixture over sausage, previously drained.
Serve with string beans and mashed potatoes.

Veal from Bagshot House

4 lbs. stewing veal, cut into   4 springs parsley
   bite-size chunks   10 bruised peppercorns
2 large onions, studded with   4 tsp. salt
   cloves   10 tbs. sweet butter
$\frac{1}{2}$ cup chopped carrots (not too $\frac{1}{2}$ lb. mushrooms
   fine)   6 tbs. flour
2 bay leaves   4 tbs. lemon juice
2 sprigs thyme, *or*   4 egg yolks
$\frac{1}{2}$ tsp. thyme to taste   2 tbs. parsley, finely chopped
24 small white pearl onions,   (optional)
   blanched

Place veal in large saucepan or pot. Add 2 quarts boiling water. Add onions, carrots, bay leaves, thyme, parsley, peppercorns and salt. Cook over low heat until veal is tender (about one hour). Strain and reserve veal stock.

While veal is cooking, cook the blanched pearl onions in 4 table-spoonfuls of the butter until tender (about 20 minutes). Wipe mushrooms with a damp paper towel, slice and cook in a small amount of the reserved veal stock for about 5 minutes.

Melt remaining 6 tablespoonfuls of butter in a saucepan and add all the flour, stirring to make a paste and add 5 cups of the strained reserved veal stock. Simmer until thick, stirring constantly.

Add lemon juice to the egg yolks. Combine and beat with a little of the hot sauce. Stir into thickened sauce. Add veal, mushrooms and onions.

Sprinkle with parsley. Serve with rice or new potatoes. Serves 8–10.

Suggested wine: Beaujolais St Andre

Baked ham

shoulder or butt ham
1 large can pineapple slices

2 cans Pepsi-Cola
cloves

Place ham in baking pan and cover ham with pineapple slices and cloves. Pour Pepsi-Cola completely over ham and place in oven at 350°F for 2 hours, basting constantly.

Serve with mashed potatoes, carrots and peas.

Pork chops from Bridgetown

12 pork chops
salt
pepper
$\frac{1}{2}$ tbs. thyme
1 tbs. sugar
1 bottle chilli sauce

$\frac{1}{2}$ bottle onion barbeque sauce
1 tbs. A–1 steak sauce
1 tbs. Worcestershire sauce
$\frac{1}{2}$ tsp. Tabasco sauce
1 large onion, sliced into rings
1 stick butter, cut into chunks

Mix together salt, pepper, thyme, sugar and sauces; blend well. Place pork chops in large baking pan and cover with onions and butter. Cook at 350°F for one hour, covered. Serve with noodles. Serves 6.

Suggested wine: Puligny-Montrachet

Babb's Pepsi kitchen sauté of veal Marengo

Cut up veal. Fry in butter with chopped onion and garlic. Add white wine, brown gravy sauce, diced tomatoes, pearl onions, and mushrooms.
Cook in oven for $1\frac{1}{2}$ hours at 350°F. Garnish with a heart-shaped croutons.

Rockley veal marsala

veal escalope
Marsala wine (white wine)
butter
cream, fresh

chopped parsley
salt and pepper
sliced mushrooms

Flour escalope. Place butter in frying pan, and when foaming, put in escalope, sauté until cooked. Take out of pan, place on to serving dish. Add mushrooms. Swill pan with wine, add cream, pour over escalope. Sprinkle with plenty of chopped parsley.

Veal cutlets Barbados style

6 veal cutlets
$\frac{1}{2}$ cup white cooking wine
salt
pepper
$\frac{1}{2}$ tsp. thyme
$\frac{1}{2}$ tsp. curry powder
$\frac{1}{2}$ tsp. chicken poultry seasoning

$\frac{1}{2}$ tsp. garlic powder
1 tbs. kitchen bouquet
$\frac{1}{4}$ tbs. cloves
2 eggs
$\frac{1}{4}$ cup milk
1 cup breadcrumbs
Crisco cooking oil

Soak cutlets in wine for about 25 minutes and reserve wine when through. In the meanwhile, prepare a batter of eggs, milk and seasonings (salt, pepper, curry, poultry seasoning, garlic powder, cloves and kitchen bouquet) and mix well. Dredge veal cutlets in batter and dip each cutlet in breadcrumbs, covering well. Brown cutlets in skillet of Crisco. Remove cutlets; place in ovenproof dish and cook at 350°F for about 30 minutes covered in original wine used for soaking. Serve with mashed potatoes and string beans. Serves 6.

Dessert suggestion: Fresh fruit salad
Wine suggestion: Beaujolais St Andre, 1971

Babb's veal cutlet delight

veal cutlet   garlic salt
black pepper   dry thyme

Bread veal cutlet, fry in deep fryer. Add 2 large sliced onions and 3 large tomatoes
After frying, put layer of onion in pan, add cutlet, add layer of tomato and another layer of onion. Add ingredients below to meat and cover with aluminum foil.

1 tblsp. A–1 Sauce $\frac{1}{2}$ tsp. Gravy Master
1 tblsp. Worcestershire sauce   1 stick butter
                                1 glass of sherry

Place in oven at 350°F for approximately 30 minutes.
Serve with mashed potatoes or rice, string beans, sliced beets.

Soup: Cream of Celery
Dessert: Assorted pies
Beverage: White wine

Curried goat from Jamaica

(For basement party disco)

6–8 lbs. of goat meat, chopped
   up
2 cups mayonnaise
juice of 1 lemon
salt
1 tsp. garlic salt

1 tsp. black pepper
2 large white onions, chopped
2 cloves of fresh garlic
3 heaped tbsp. curry powder
1 cup cooking oil

Mix mayonnaise, salt and lemon juice together and soak meat in mixture for $\frac{1}{2}$ hour. Add garlic salt, black pepper, onions, and garlic and fry very slowly in oil. Add curry powder and cook until tender. Serve with plain Carolina rice, Jamaican strong rum, chased with Pepsi-Cola, Mountain Dew and iced water.

Soup: Cream of Corn

Babb's homemade liver

liver
salt and pepper
bread crumbs
flour
eggs

bacon
mashed potatoes
peas
cauliflower

Sprinkle salt and pepper on liver. Combine breadcrumbs and flour together, beat egg, dip liver in egg and then in breadcrumb and flour mixture. Fry with low flame in oil until golden brown.
Serve with crisp bacon, mashed potatoes, peas, and cauliflower.

Soup: Cream of Potato
Beverage: Pepsi-Cola
Dessert: Fresh pineapple (add 1 cup of chilled Harvey's Bristol Cream sherry before serving)

Chef Babb's complete 'Chicken of the island' dinner

3 lbs. of chicken – cut into pieces
5 tblsp. margarine or oil
6 tomatoes
3 green peppers
3 onions
3 cloves garlic

$\frac{1}{8}$ tsp. cayenne pepper *or*
$\frac{1}{4}$ tsp. black pepper
$\frac{1}{4}$ tsp. Tabasco
$\frac{1}{4}$ tsp. thyme
1 tblsp. tomato ketchup
$\frac{1}{4}$ tsp. dry mustard
$\frac{1}{4}$ tsp. horseradish sauce

Plunge tomatoes into boiling water, then into cold water and peel, cut into chunks ($\frac{1}{6}$ ths). Remove seeds from green peppers and cut into chunks. Chop onions into large pieces.

Brown chicken in the oil or margarine in a heavy pan, remove chicken and brown onions slightly. Replace chicken in the pan over onions and add tomatoes, green peppers and the remaining ingredients. Simmer for about 40 minutes, with the cover slightly off the pan, allowing some air to enter. Serves 4–6.

Serve with plain rice, frozen Brussels sprouts and a chilled white wine, followed by fresh fruit and finish with a demi-tasse and a nightcap.

Soup: Vegetable

Caribbean chicken paprika

Marinate 8 chicken legs for $\frac{1}{2}$ hour in lemon juice and salt. Wash chicken legs and place in baking pan. Put 2 big onions and 6 large tomatoes (both sliced) on top of the chicken and add:

1 can mushroom soup
1 can tomato soup
$\frac{1}{2}$ tsp. garlic salt
$\frac{1}{2}$ tsp. garlic powder

1 stick butter
2 jiggers of wine
6 cubes of chicken bouillon
sprinkle of paprika

Cover with foil and bake at 350°F for 1 hour.
Serve with rice, cut green beans and tossed salad.

Soup: Cream of Chicken
Dessert: Banana Flambé
Peel bananas and sprinkle with sugar and cinnamon. Place butter in pan and saute tó brown. Place in serving dish, pour brandy or rum on top and serve.
Beverage: Frozen Daiquiri

Roast chicken from the Pepsi Executive Kitchen

Perdue roaster chicken

Soak chicken in lemon juice and salt for $\frac{1}{2}$ hour, then rinse. Put foil on bottom of roasting pan. Place chicken in roasting pan.
Sprinkle black pepper, garlic salt, dried thyme over chicken. Add 2 cubes of chicken boullion per chicken.
Place $\frac{1}{2}$ tsp. garlic salt, $\frac{1}{2}$ tsp. garlic powder, $\frac{1}{2}$ tsp. black pepper inside chicken. Place wedge of butter on end of chicken. Dice small onion and put into pan around chicken. Cover with foil. Bake at 400°F for 1 hour. Lower oven to 350°F, remove foil and baste until brown.
Serve with wild rice and mixed peas and corn.

Soup: Chicken Noodle
Dessert: Rice pudding
Beverage: While Yago

Babb's sautéed chicken

Place chicken breasts in pan. Squeeze 2 whole lemons on chicken. Marinate for $\frac{1}{2}$ hour. Wash off lemon and add $\frac{1}{2}$ tsp. garlic salt and powder, $\frac{1}{2}$ tsp. dry tyme, $\frac{1}{2}$ tsp. black pepper, 1 glass of sherry. Place chicken in broiler with herbs on top. Baste with sherry, add mushrooms and cook for 25 minutes.

Babb's southern fried chicken

Chicken breasts or legs

Place chicken breasts or legs in salt and lemon for 45 minutes. Rinse chicken and place in large pan.
Sprinkle dried thyme, black pepper, garlic salt and garlic pepper, to taste, over chicken.
Put generous amount of Crisco oil in frying pan and get oil hot. Lower flame when hot and dip chicken into beaten egg and then into breadcrumb and flour mixture. Drop into frying pan gently and fry until golden brown.

Split peas and rice

Boil water and add ham hock and a small onion. Boil for 25 minutes. Sprinkle dried thyme and add green split peas. Cook for 5 minutes. Add rice (cook accordingly – Uncle Ben's preferred). Gradually add juice from chicken after rice is absorbed.

Serve with green salad

Soup: Chicken Gumbo
Dessert: Pie à la mode
Beverage: White wine

Ali Babb's turkey breast curry for Thanksgiving

1 jar of chutney
turkey breast, cut up
2 sticks of butter for frying pan
$\frac{1}{2}$ tsp. thyme
$\frac{1}{2}$ tsp. black pepper
1 tsp. garlic salt
1 head of celery, chopped

1 large can of tomato purée
8 packages of chicken broth
1 tsp. salt
2 tblsp. of Worcestershire sauce
1 bottle of A–1 sauce
1 bottle of ketchup
1 tsp. of Tabasco

4 large green peppers, chopped
3 tblsp. of curry powder

Mix ingredients, place in frying pan and cook for one hour.
Serve with rice, green tossed salad and trimmings of coconut, peanuts (crushed), raisins, bananas, chopped cauliflower, broccoli, sweet pepper and chutney, each in separate bowls
Serve with white wine

Soup: Split Pea with Croutons
Dessert: Fresh fruit salad, cheesecake or pecan pie.
Coffee

Babb's original turkey-pasta casserole

$\frac{1}{2}$ turkey breast, diced
2 large onions, diced
4 stalks of celery, diced
3 lbs. can of whole tomatoes
1 box of elbow macaroni (24 oz. or larger)
1 box of frozen peas (2 lbs.)
2 large sweet peppers
$\frac{1}{2}$ tsp. thyme

$\frac{1}{2}$ tsp. black pepper
$\frac{1}{2}$ tsp. salt
4 packages of chicken bouillon
1 tbl. A–1 Sauce
1 tsp. Worcestershire sauce
1 bottle of ketchup
1 jigger of sherry
1 stick of butter
grated cheese

Place butter in frying pan with onions and all the ingredients. Mix in the can of tomatoes and turkey.
Boil macaroni until cooked. Boil peas until cooked. Mix peas and macaroni together with other ingredients. Place in casserole dish. Bake for 25 minutes at 350°F with grated cheese sprinkled on top.

Serve with spinach salad:

spinach
mushrooms
red cabbage
chopped celery

red sweet pepper
crisp bacon, chopped up
Wishbone Italian dressing

Sprinkle chopped hard-boiled egg on top before serving.

Suggested Wine: Monsieur Henri Meursault white wine.
Dessert: Fresh fruit salad. Coffee.

Turkey à la Roma

$\frac{1}{2}$ turkey breast
2 large onions, diced
1 head celery, diced
4 green peppers
2 cups of carrots, diced
2 sticks butter
1 large can of tomato paste
8 large potatoes, cooked and
   mashed

4 packages of beef bouillon
$\frac{1}{2}$ tsp. dry thyme
$\frac{1}{2}$ tsp. black pepper
1 can of mushroom soup
1 can of tomato soup
1 jigger of Harvey's Bristol
   Cream sherry
grated cheese

Sauté the onions, celery and peppers with the butter and add herbs, tomato paste, beef bouillon, tomato soup, and mushroom soup. Add carrots to bottom of casserole dish, then add turkey, and place potatoes on top of casserole. Place in 350°F oven with cheese on top to brown.
Serve with a tossed salad and white wine.

Dessert: Fresh strawberries sprinkled with sugar and three jiggers of Harvey's Bristol Cream sherry.

Chilli chicken from Tobago

1 whole chicken
lemon
salt
pepper
finely chopped onion
finely chopped celery
butter

Sauce mix
1 bottle chilli sauce
1 tbs. kitchen bouquet
1 tsp. A–1 sauce
1 tsp. Worcestershire sauce
$\frac{1}{8}$ tsp. thyme

Preheat oven to 300°F. Soak chicken in lemon with salt for 25 minutes. Rinse and pat dry. Place chicken in baking dish; add salt and pepper, cover with chopped onion and chopped celery. Cover with sauce mix and add a few pats of butter. Bake for approximately one hour.

Suggested wine: Puligny-Montrachet

Chicken in wine from St Thomas

1 chicken, cut up   parsley
1 cup white wine   2 tbs. olive oil
1 clove garlic   salt and pepper to taste

Pour the oil in a frying pan and add chicken with garlic, salt, pepper and parsley; cook until chicken is brown. When browned well, add wine and simmer for $\frac{3}{4}$ of an hour. Serves 4.

Suggested wine: Marques de Murrieta

Babb's chicken supreme

1 whole chicken   1 package frozen peas
$\frac{3}{4}$ lb. fresh mushrooms   1 package frozen sliced carrots
2 cans mushroom soup $\frac{1}{2}$ tsp. thyme
2 sweet peppers   1 tbs. sherry
$\frac{1}{2}$ head celery $\frac{1}{2}$ dry mustard
1 large onion   1 tsp. Worcestershire sauce
$\frac{1}{2}$ cup butter   1 tsp. A–1 sauce

Wash the chicken in lemon juice before placing in pan with water. Chop one pepper, $\frac{1}{2}$ onion and two stalks celery; add to water to be used for cooking chicken. Cook until tender and let cool. Chop $\frac{1}{2}$ onion, one pepper and rest of celery; sauté with butter until tender. Add mushrooms previously chopped in large pieces and the sherry, and simmer until tender.

Meanwhile, remove cooled chicken, take off skin and cut meat into chunks. Use leftover water to cook peas and carrots for about ten minutes; strain. Go back to mushroom mixture, add mushroom soup and thyme, mustard. Worcestershire and A–1 sauces; simmer a few minutes, stirring well.

In glass baking dish, place alternate layers of sauce with chicken chunks and vegetables. Place in 300°F oven for about 20 minutes, with lid on. Serve with salad. Serves approximately 6.

Suggested wine: Puligny Montrachet

Baked marinaded chicken breasts from Barbados

8 chicken breasts   garlic powder
salt   1 bottle of Milani's 1890 French
pepper   dressing

Lightly season chicken breasts with salt, pepper and garlic powder. Marinate chicken breasts in French dressing for at least 4 hours, turning frequently. Bake in 325°F oven for $1\frac{1}{4}$ hours. Turn every 20 minutes. Serves 4.

Dalton Manor sauce

1 pint vegetable oil   2 oz. fresh mustard
$\frac{1}{3}$ pint Worcestershire sauce   freshly ground pepper
$\frac{1}{3}$ pint tarragon vinegar   salt
1 grated onion

Mix all ingredients together. Brush chicken with sauce and baste occasionally during cooking process.

Stuffed chicken from Grenada

1 4lb. broiler chicken	$\frac{1}{2}$ tsp. thyme
juice from $\frac{1}{2}$ lemon	$\frac{1}{2}$ tsp. black pepper
$\frac{1}{2}$ tsp. salt	$\frac{1}{4}$ tsp. garlic powder
1 lb. pork sausage, cut up	$\frac{1}{4}$ tsp. cloves
8 oz. seasoned breadcrumbs	$\frac{1}{2}$ cup white wine
2 stalks celery, diced	$\frac{1}{2}$ tsp. thyme
1 small onion, diced	$\frac{1}{2}$ tsp. black pepper
1 stick butter	$\frac{1}{2}$ tsp. poultry seasoning

Rub chicken with lemon juice and salt, set aside for 25 minutes and then thoroughly rinse. Dry with paper towel.

In a large frying pan, melt butter and add sausage and gradually add breadcrumbs, celery, onions, thyme, pepper, garlic powder, cloves and wine. Cook over medium heat until browned.

Sprinkle the additional thyme and pepper and poultry seasoning inside the chicken, in the meantime. Then stuff the sausage mixture into chicken, cover with aluminium foil and bake in 400°F oven for about two hours. After $1\frac{1}{2}$ hours cooking, remove foil and baste chicken with drippings. Serve with sliced carrots and salad. Serves 4.

Suggested wine: Weber Moselblumchen

Bagshot House sweet and sour stuffing

(for chicken, etc.)

4 lbs. sausage meat	mixed herbs
$\frac{1}{2}$ lb. seedless raisins	4 eggs
$\frac{1}{4}$ lb. chopped walnuts	chicken stock (enough to make
$\frac{1}{2}$ lb. chopped gherkins	mixture moist)

Mix ingredients together and use to stuff poultry for roasting.

Craig's alley sauce

4 onions sliced thinly
12 ozs. mushrooms, sliced
6 tomatoes (skinned seeded
  and chopped)
6 ozs. seedless raisins

6 oranges (grated rind and
  juice)
1 dstsp. lime juice
6 ozs. Madeira wine
2 ozs. cornflour
2 pints duck stock

Cook mushrooms and onions in a little duck fat for 4–5 minutes. Add stock and rest of ingredients, simmer gently for a few minutes. Thicken with cornflour mixed with a little cold water.

7 Desserts and Cakes

Coffee toffee pie

Pastry shell

$\frac{1}{2}$ package pie crust mix
$\frac{1}{4}$ cup light brown sugar,
  firmly packed
$\frac{3}{4}$ cup finely chopped walnuts

1 square unsweetened
  chocolate, grated
1 tsp. vanilla extract

Preheat oven to 375°F. In a medium bowl, combine everything with one tablespoon water. Using fork, mix well and blend. Put in well-greased, 9″ pie plate and press firmly against bottom and sides of pie plate. Bake for 15 minutes.

Filling

$\frac{1}{2}$ cup butter, softened
$\frac{3}{4}$ cup granulated sugar
1 square unsweetened
  chocolate, melted

2 tsp. instant coffee
3 eggs

In a small bowl with electric mixer, beat butter until creamy. Gradually add sugar. Beat until light. Blend in cooled melted chocolate and instant coffee. Add one egg at a time and beat for five minutes between each egg (total 15 minutes.) Turn into baked pie shell and refrigerate pie overnight, covered.

Topping

2 cups heavy cream
2 tsp. instant coffee

$\frac{1}{2}$ cup confectioner's sugar

Let above ingredients stand in refrigerator for one hour after combining. After that, beat until stiff. Put topping over filling and let stand for two hours in refrigerator. Garnish with chocolate curls.

Coconut/lemon Pepsi cake

$\frac{1}{2}$ cup butter
1 cup sugar
6 eggs
1 tsp. salt
2 cups flour
2 tsp. baking powder
$\frac{1}{2}$ cup milk

$\frac{2}{3}$ cup Pepsi
1 cup raisins
3 tsp. cherry preserve
rind of one fresh lemon
1 tsp. rum extract
$3\frac{1}{2}$ oz. shredded coconut
1 tsp. cinnamon

Cream butter and sugar. Add eggs one at a time, beating well after each addition. Add flour, baking powder and salt (sifted together) alternately with milk and Pepsi. Add raisins, cherry preserve, lemon rind, rum extract, and coconut.
Mix well. Bake in well-greased baking pan at 350°F for one hour. Serve with whipped cream topping.

Chocolate mousse

$\frac{1}{4}$ lb. sweet butter, softened
2 lbs. semi-sweet chocolate
4 egg yolks

4 egg whites, beaten
1 pint heavy cream, whipped

Melt chocolate over double boiler. Remove from heat and add butter and egg yolks. Stir well until combined. Cool. Add beaten egg whites and whipped cream; fold in until well combined. Chill until firm. Serve with whipped cream.

Babb's homemade noodle pudding

1 lb. broad noodles
salt
1 lemon
4 eggs
$\frac{1}{4}$ lb. butter

1 cup brown sugar
cinnamon
$\frac{1}{2}$ cup blanched, slivered or
    sliced almonds

Cook noodles in salted water and drain in cold water. Squeeze lemon; mix juice with noodles and eggs. Melt butter and add brown sugar. Cook until it forms a paste.
Put sugar mixture in bottom of a well-greased 12-inch ring mould. Sprinkle cinnamon over sugar. Add noodle mix, and sprinkle almonds over mixture.
Bake in moderate oven (325°F) for 45 minutes.

Chocolate Pixies

4 packs unsweetened
   chocolate (Nestle's)
$2\frac{1}{2}$ cups sifted flour
2 tsp. baking powder
$\frac{1}{2}$ tsp. salt

$\frac{1}{2}$ cup vegetable oil
2 cups sugar
2 tsp. vanilla
4 eggs
1 cup confectioner's sugar

Sift together flour, baking powder and salt. Combine oil, chocolate and sugar. Add eggs one at a time and beat well after each egg. Add vanilla. Add sifted dry ingredients to chocolate mixture and blend thoroughly; chill overnight.
Heat oven to 350°F. Lightly grease cookie sheet with unsalted shortening. Spread confectioner's sugar on waxed paper or in a small flat pan, and drop dough in rounded teaspoonfuls into sugar. With fingers, coat dough with sugar and roll into small balls. Place two inches apart and bake for 10–20 minutes.
Cool slightly and remove to cool. Store in airtight container for one week or one month in freezer. Makes six dozen.

Fresh strawberries 'n melon

5- quarts strawberries   2 quarts sour cream
1 large honeydew melon $\frac{1}{2}$ cup sugar

Clean strawberries. Cut melon into bite-size pieces. Add sour cream
and sugar.

Jam creamettes

$2\frac{3}{4}$ cups sifted flour   red jam
$1\frac{1}{2}$ cups heavy cream   confectioner's sugar
pinch salt   granulated sugar
1 cup soft butter

In electric mixer or with wooden spoon mix flour, salt, cream and
butter until well blended and chill several hours or until very firm.
Roll on sugared board to $\frac{1}{8}''$ thickness. Cut half the dough in circles
and the other half with doughnut cutter. Bake at 350°F for about
8 minutes. Cool on racks. Put teaspoon of jam in centre of circles and
cover with doughnut-cut rings. Sprinkle with sugar.

Candy canes

$3\frac{1}{4}$ cups sifted flour   1 egg
4 tsp. baking powder $\frac{1}{2}$ tsp. peppermint extract
1 tsp. salt $\frac{1}{4}$ cup milk
$\frac{1}{2}$ cup butter   red food colouring
$1\frac{1}{4}$ cups sugar

Sift flour, baking powder and salt onto wax paper. Beat butter and
sugar in large bowl until fluffy, beat in egg and peppermint extract.
Stir in flour mixture alternately with milk. Spoon half the dough into
a medium size bowl; tint pink with red colouring. Leave remaining
mixture plain.

Pinch off about one teaspoon of each dough and roll into pencil-thin five-inch strips. Place strips side by side, pressing ends together and then twist. Place on ungreased cookie sheet one inch apart and bend in cane shape.

Bake at 350°F for about ten minutes until firm. Cool a few minutes on cookie sheet and remove carefully. Cool.

Snow drops

1 cup butter	1 cup chopped walnuts
4 tbs. confectioner's sugar	2 tsp. vanilla
2 cups sifted flour	1 tsp. water

Blend butter until creamy and add sugar. Stir in flour and blend well. Add chopped nuts, vanilla and water. Chill one hour. Roll into small balls. Bake on ungreased cookie sheet at 350°F for 10–12 minutes. Do not brown. Roll in confectioner's sugar while hot.

Russian tea cakes

2 cups sweet butter	1 jigger brandy or cognac
$\frac{3}{4}$ cup confectioner's sugar	$4\frac{1}{2}$ cups sifted flour
1 egg yolk	chopped walnuts

Cream butter very lightly, gradually beating in sugar. Beat in egg yolk and brandy. Blend in flour slowly to make dough soft. With floured hands, shape dough into one-inch balls. In blender, chop walnuts until very fine, and roll balls in nuts. Place on baking sheet and bake at 350°F for 15 minutes. Cool slightly and place in cupcake papers. Sift confectioner's sugar over cakes lightly.

Cream cheese cookies

2 cups sifted flour	1 cup sugar
1 cup butter, softened	1 egg yolk
3 oz. package cream cheese	1 tsp. vanilla extract

Mix together butter and cream cheese and stir in sugar. Beat until fluffy and add vanilla. Stir in flour and egg yolk; mix well, put through cookie press.
Bake at 375°F until lightly browned.

Vienna crescents

1 cup sweet butter, softened	2 tsp. vanilla
2 cups sifted flour	1 cup chopped almonds
1 cup sugar	confectioner's sugar
$\frac{1}{4}$ tsp. salt	

Heat oven to 300°F. Work butter and sugar in a bowl until creamy. Add flour, salt, vanilla and nuts. Mix until well blended. Shape crescents with one teaspoon dough. Place one inch apart on cookie sheet and bake for 18–20 minutes. Cool slightly and roll in confectioner's sugar.

Fruit soup

2 pints water	3 ozs. seedless raisins
4 ozs. sugar	juice of 3 lemons
8 ozs. sweet pitted cherries	3 pints orange juice
8 ozs. peaches	6 ozs. cold water
6 ozs. maraschino cherries	$1\frac{1}{2}$ ozs. cornstarch
1 × 27 ozs. can mandarin oranges and juice	

Bring the two pints of water to boil, add sugar and dissolve. Add fruit and lemon juice. Return to boil. Reduce heat. Bring orange juice to boil. Blend cold water and cornstarch add to orange juice. When thickened add orange juice to fruit. Stir gently. Chill overnight.

Christmas fruit cake

1 lb apples, or any other fresh
   or canned fruit
5 oz. flour

5 oz. sugar
3 eggs
1 cup of milk

Peel apples and cut into thin slices.
In a mixing bowl, combine flour, sugar and eggs. Mix well. Add slightly warmed milk and mix gently.
Place the sliced apples in a buttered baking dish and cover with the mixture. Bake at 350°F for 45 minutes.

Fruit topping Tobago

3 eggs, slightly beaten
$\frac{3}{4}$ cup brown sugar
$\frac{1}{2}$ cup orange juice

3 tbsp. fresh lemon juice
1 tbsp. grated grapefruit peel
$1\frac{1}{2}$ cups sour cream

Combine eggs, brown sugar and orange juice in a saucepan. Cook over medium heat, stirring until thickened. Remove from heat. Blend in lemon juice and grapefruit peel and cool. Mix in sour cream (gently). Cover and chill.

Suggested fruits (all fresh)
cantelope
honeydew
strawberries
bananas
blueberries
seedless black grapes

Bagshot House dessert soufflé

6 eggs, separated
pinch of salt
2 tbsp. flour

4 oz. butter
$2\frac{1}{2}$ tbsp. sugar

Beat the six egg whites with salt until very stiff. Add sugar gradually while beating. Lightly fold in only 2 of the yolks, slightly beaten. Do not stir. Melt butter in a baking dish or soufflé dish. Add the egg mixture to the hot butter without stirring and place in 350°F oven. Bake for 7–10 minutes until golden brown. *Do not open oven door during baking*! Dust with powdered sugar and serve immediately. Can also be topped with jam or jelly.

Executive's dining room dessert

1 honeydew melon (large)
5 pear halves (canned)
5 peach halves (canned)

1 package strawberry jello
1 cup milk

Cut melon in half and remove seeds. Prepare jello by using one cup hot water and one cup of cold milk. Place peaches and pears in centre of melon and pour prepared jello over fruit.
Refrigerate until gelled before serving.

8 Special Menus

Babb's dinner menu (1)

A cocktail of melon, cucumber and pimento
Egg mousse with caviar and sour cream sauce
Spaghetti Bolognaise
Banana and chopped nuts salad
Buttered corn on the cob

*

Cream of spinach soup
Chilled orange and tomato soup

*

Kebab of seafood with rice, together with a spicy sauce

*

Escalope of veal with lemon juice, egg and parsley
Saddle of lamb roasted with rosemary
Cornish game hen cooked with red wine and baby onions
Cream cheese and chive pancake
Cold roast chicken and salad
Fresh local lobster grilled with butter

*

An assortment of vegetables

*

Mixed salad bowl

*

A selection of desserts from the trolley

*

Various ice creams   Paradise parfait

*

Cheese board   Dinner mints
Coffee

*

Recommended wines

Pouilley Fume   Rosatello
Chateauneuf du Pape

Babb's dinner menu (2)

Baked christophene with lemon chicken
Avocado mousse with Creole dressing
Seasoned seafood cocktail
Half a grapefruit grilled with rum and brown sugar
Chef's homemade liver pate with toast

*

French onion soup
Chilled cucumber soup

*

A scallop of shellfish with Tamarind sauce

*

Grilled entrecote steak, peppered or with garlic
A tender gammon rasher with creamy parsley sauce
Roast Norfolk turkey with a whisky and orange sauce
Mushroom omelette
Cold ox tongue and salad
Fresh local lobster grilled with butter

*

An assortment of vegetables

*

Mixed salad bowl

*

A selection of desserts from the trolley

*

Various ice creams   Coupe St James

*

Cheese board   Dinner mints
Coffee

*

Recommended wines

Chilean Burgundy   Rose d'Anjou
Soave

Babb's dinner menu (3)

Cucumber, cheese and olives on a skewer with an avocado dip
Sliced eggplant covered in a seasoned tomato sauce and Parmesan
cheese
Melon and seafood cocktail
A whole tomato filled with minced beef, diced mushrooms and sweet
pepper
An open pancake with a quiche filling

*

Shrimp soup
Chilled lettuce and carrot soup

*

Grilled red snapper with nut brown butter and lime tips

*

Braised fresh ox-tongue with caper sauce
Roast leg of pork with sage and lime sauce and seasoned stuffing
Crispy chicken served with a piquant and cinnamon dip
Spinach omelette
Cold roast beef and salad

*

An assortment of vegetables

*

Mixed salad bowl

*

A selection of desserts from the trolley

*

Various ice creams   Banana sundae

*

Cheese board   Dinner mints
Coffee

*

Recommended wines

Valpolicella   Mateus Rosé
Vina Sol

Babb's dinner menu (4)

Egg patties with tarragon sauce
Green peppers filled with eggplant and garlic
Caribbean fruit cup with rum and honey sauce
Spiced ham mousse with mustard dressing
Bajan shrimp cocktail

*

Consommé brunoise
Chilled avocado soup

*

Sauteed kingfish Arawak with banana and pineapple

*

Spiced roast chicken with prune and rosemary stuffing
Whole fillet of beef sliced and cooked with a piquant sauce
Pork chops marinated in thyme and cooked with white wine and
gherkins
Fines herbes omelette
Cold roast lamb and salad
Fresh local lobster grilled with butter

*

An assortment of vegetables

*

Mixed salad bowl

*

Fresh fruit salad   Various ice creams
Black Forest gâteau   Lime soufflé
Coconut meringue   Individual fruit tartlets
Peach melba

*

Cheese board   Dinner mints
Coffee

*

Recommended wines

Beaujolais   Muscadet
Rose d'Anjou

Babb's dinner menu (5)

A cocktail of melon, cucumber and pimento
Seasoned seafood cocktail
Chef's home made liver pate with toast
Egg patties with tarragon sauce

*

French onion soup
Chilled cucumber soup

*

Grilled fillet of marlin with lime butter and chopped shallots
Minute steak Provençale
Roast chicken with bacon and bread sauce
Mushroom or plain omelette
Cold roast lamb and salad

*

A selection of vegetables

*

Mixed salad bowl

*

Desserts from the trolley

*

Various ice creams

*

Cheese board   Dinner mints
Coffee

*

Recommended wines

Mateus Rose   Pouilly Fuisse
Mouton Cadet Rouge

Babb's dinner menu (6)

Green peppers filled with savoury eggplant and a touch of garlic
Caribbean fruit cup with rum and honey sauce
Spiced ham mousse with mustard dressing
Bajan shrimp cocktail

*

Local fish chowder
Iced curry soup

*

Sautéed kingfish Arawak with pineapple and banana
Spiced roast chicken with prune and rosemary stuffing
Whole fillet of beef sliced and cooked with a piquant sauce
Fines herbs or plain omelette
Cold baked ham and salad

*

A selection of vegetables

*

Mixed salad bowl

*

Desserts from the trolley

*

Various ice creams

*

Cheese board   Dinner mints
Coffee

*

Recommended wines

Le Chaillou   Mateus Rose
Piesporter

Babb's dinner menu (7)

A cocktail of melon, cucumber and pimento
Seasoned seafood cocktail
Chef's home-made liver pate with toast
Egg patties with tarragon sauce

*

French onion soup
Chilled cucumber soup

*

Grilled marlin with lime butter and chopped shallots
Braised fresh ox tongue with Caper sauce
Roast Norfolk turkey with stuffing and orange sauce
Mushroom or plain omelette
Cold roast lamb and salad

*

A selection of vegetables

*

Mixed salad bowl

*

Desserts from the trolley

*

Various ice creams

*

Cheese board   Dinner mints
Coffee

*

Recommended wines

Chilean Burgundy   Soave
Rose d'Anjou

Babb's dinner menu (8)

Chicken livers wrapped in bacon
A variety of Caribbean seafood in a piquant sauce
Avocado mousse with a delicately flavoured grapefruit mayonnaise

*

Cream of pumpkin soup
Chilled gazpacho

*

Grilled fillet of dolphin with olive, egg and caper sauce
Rack of lamb, roasted with rosemary and garlic
Poached chicken cooked in tarragon, sherry and tomato sauce
Mushroom omelette
Cold roast beef and salad

*

Buttered leaf spinach   Christophene au gratin
Breadfruit and beer sauce   Marquise potatoes
Mixed salad bowl

*

Fresh fruit salad   Various ice creams
Cream caramel
Strawberry gâteau   Lemon meringue pie

*

Cheese board   Dinner mints
Coffee

*

Recommended wines

Beaujolais   Rosatello
Ruppertsberger

Babb's Bajan buffet

Chilled guava nectar

*

Selection of local Fruits

*

Home-made dolphin chowder
Chilled lime consommé

*

Fried fillet of flying fish with lime tips
Baked whole kingfish with tartare sauce
Macaroni and cheese pie

*

Caribbean shrimp curry with rice and condiments
Braised chicken legs with sweet corn
Roast baron of beef with Yorkshire pudding
Baked jacket potatoes
Creole okras   Baked pumpkin au gratin
Buttered marrow   Creamed yam

*

Assorted salads

*

Choice of Sweets from the dessert table

*

Cheese board   Dinner mints
Coffee

*

Recommended wines

Chambertin Clos de Beze   Pouilly Fuisse
Mateus Rose

Babb's Caribbean surprise dinner

Chef's home-made king fish paté
Eggs filled with onions and covered with a mornay sauce
Grapefruit segments bound in yoghurt and sprinkled with nutmeg
and cinnamon
Chicken livers wrapped in bacon
Creamed mushroom tartlet

*

Fresh okra soup
Chilled cucumber, radish and fresh mint soup

*

Grilled fillet of dolphin almondine

*

Roast leg of lamb with a herb marinade
Supreme of chicken with citrus and tarragon sauce
Sautéed kidneys with sherry and cream
Fresh local lobster grilled with butter

*

A selection of vegetables

*

Mixed salad bowl

*

Desserts from the trolley

*

Pear Belle Helen
Various ice creams

*

Coffee

*

Recommended wines

Mateus Rose   Mâcon Blanc
Sangre de Toro

Babb's Bagshot House buffet

Chilled soursop nectar

*

Selection of local fruits

*

Home-made lobster bisque
Chilled grapefruit consommé

*

Breaded fillet of flying fish with lime tips
Baked whole marlin with tartare sauce
Savoury macaroni pie

*

Caribbean shrimp with sweet and sour sauce
Braised chicken legs with savoury rice
Roast baron of beef with Yorkshire pudding

*

Baked jacket potatoes
Okras and beer sauce   Eggplant fritters
Marrow au gratin   Orange sweet potatoes
Assorted salads

*

Choice of Sweets from the dessert table

*

Dinner mints
Guava cheese

*

Various ice creams

*

Coffee

*

Recommended wines

Le Chaillou   Chateau de Selle
Auxey-Duresses

Babb's West Indian buffet

Chilled tropical nectar

*

Selection of local fruits

*

Cream of breadfruit soup
Chilled sweet pepper soup

*

Fried fillet of flying fish Bajan style
Baked whole kingfish with tartare sauce
Macaroni and cheese pie

*

Caribbean shrimp creole with rice
Braised chicken legs with pineapple chunks
Roast baron of beef with Yorkshire pudding

*

Baked jacket potatoes
Okras and tomatoes   Baked pumpkin au gratin
Savoury cassava   Creamed yam
Assorted salads

*

Choice of Sweets from the dessert table

*

Cheese board   Dinner mints
Guava cheese

*

Coffee

*

Recommended wines

Chateau Boutet   Chateau Duplessis
St Emilion

Babb's special chef's salad

Salad greens, julienne ham,
Julienne turkey, julienne American cheese tossed together
and garnished with tomato and egg wedges
and green olives

*

Rolls and butter

*

German chocolate cake

*

Sodas, coffee and tea

Babb's
birthday dinner

Cream of celery soup

*

Glazed chicken garnished with sweet pepper and lettuce
Cauliflower and broccoli au gratin
Split peas and rice

*

Beef stew with carrots

*

Macaroni pie

*

Sliced tomatoes
Tossed salad (optional)
Fresh papaya with red or white wine

Babb's Saturday night buffet

Chilled guava nectar

*

Selection of local fruits

*

Fresh dolphin chowder
Chilled orange consommé

*

Breaded fillet of flying fish with lime tips
Baked whole kingfish with tartare sauce
Macaroni and cheese pie

*

Caribbean shrimps with sweet and sour sauce
Braised chicken legs with savoury rice
Roast baron of beef with Yorkshire pudding

*

Baked jacket potatoes
Okras and beer sauce   Buttered sliced beets
Steamed pumpkin   Creamed yam
Assorted salads

*

Choice of Sweets from the dessert table

*

Cheese board

*

Guava cheese   Dinner mints
Coffee

*

Recommended wines

Chateau Timberlay   Auxey-Duresses
Mateus Rose

Babb's Gold Coast Dinner

A cocktail of melon, cucumber and pimento
Egg mousse with caviar and sour cream sauce
Curried fruit served on a bed of brown rice
Buttered corn on the cob

*

Cream of spinach soup
Chilled orange and tomato soup

*

Kebab of seafood served with rice and a spicy sauce

*

Escalope of veal with lemon juice, egg and parsley
(6 lbs of veal)
Leg of lamb roasted with rosemary
Cornish game hen cooked with red wine and baby onions
Cream cheese and chive pancake
Cold roast chicken and salad
Fresh local lobster grilled with butter

*

A selection of vegetables

*

Mixed salad bowl

*

Desserts from the trolley

*

Paradise parfait
Various ice creams

*

Coffee

*

Recommended wines

Any white or red wines

Babb's speciality dinner

Chef's home-made liver paté
Tuna fish, cucumber and tomato salad
Caribbean fruit cup with rum and honey sauce

*

French onion soup
Chilled avocado soup

*

Poached fillet of kingfish with yoghurt sauce and herbs
Roast chicken with bacon and bread sauce
Fillet of beef sliced and cooked in a piquant sauce
Spanish omelette
Cold baked ham and salad

*

Cauliflower au gratin   Glazed carrots
Spiced sweet potatoes   Parmentier potatoes
Mixed salad bowl

*

Fresh fruit salad   Various ice creams
Black forest gâteau   Apple strudel

*

Coffee

*

Recommended wines

Any red or white wines

Babb's Island in the Sun dinner

Buttered corn on the cob
Egg and melon boat
Curried shrimp creole

*

Cream of breadfruit soup
Chilled orange and tomato soup

*

Poached fillet of kingfish with yoghurt sauce and herbs
Roast leg of pork with sage and lime sauce and seasoned stuffing
Lamb's kidneys, button mushrooms and bacon
Grilled on a skewer and served on a bed of rice
Quiche Lorraine
Cold baked ham and salad

*

Christophene Creole   Buttered leaf spinach
Mixed salad bowl   Baked potatoes

*

Fresh fruit salad   Pecan pie
Cream puffs and chocolate sauce

*

Coffee

*

Recommended wines

Rose d'Anjou
Macon Blanc

Babb's dinner delights

Banana and chopped nut salad
Sliced eggplant covered in a seasoned tomato sauce and covered with
Parmesan cheese
Spaghetti Bolognaise

*

Fresh okra soup
Chilled cucumber soup

*

Poached fillet of flying fish filled with chopped shrimps and parsley
Grilled sirloin steak served plain or with a creamy béarnaise sauce
Sautéed veal escalope with green peppers and caper sauce
Ham and cheese omelette
Cold roast chicken and salad

*

Buttered green beans   Croquette potatoes
Spiced sweet potatoes   Mixed salad bowl

*

Black Forest cake   Lemon meringue pie

*

Cheese board   Dinner mints
Coffee

*

Recommended wines

Pinot Noir   Pinot Chardonnay
Chateau de Selle

Babb's fresh island dinner

Gingered orange, banana and pear salad
Sliced eggplant covered in a seasoned tomato sauce and
Parmesan cheese
(8 eggplants)
Melon and seafood cocktail
(1 whole melon)
A whole tomato filled with minced ham, diced mushrooms and
sweet pepper
(6 large tomatoes)
A crêpe shell with broccoli, cheese sauce and topped with bacon
*
Shrimp soup
Chilled lettuce and carrot soup
*
Grilled red snapper with nut brown butter and lime tips
(4 lbs. of snapper fillet)
*
Braised fresh ox tongue with Caper sauce
(1 ox tongue)
Roast leg of pork with sage and lime sauce and seasoned stuffing
(1 leg of pork)
Spinach omelette
*
Supplement: grilled local lobster with butter
*
An assortment of vegetables
*
Mixed salad bowl
*
A selection of desserts from the trolley
*
Various ice creams   Banana sundae
*
Coffee

*

Recommended wines

Valpolicella   Mateus rose
Vina Sol

Babb's dinner royale

Orange and grapefruit segments in a rum sauce
Curried fruit and brown rice
Spiced ham mousse with a delicately flavoured mustard dressing

*

Cream of spinach soup
Chilled cucumber, radish, yoghurt, and fresh mint soup

*

Grilled fillet of red snapper with parsley butter
Roast leg of lamb with mint sauce
Supreme of chicken in a sherry cream sauce with pimentoes and
mushrooms
A pancake filled with fresh vegetables and covered with
melted cheese
Cold baked ham and salad

*

Buttered okras   Christophene au gratin
Orange sweet potatoes   Oven roast potatoes
Mixed salad bowl

*

Fresh fruit salad   Lemon meringue pie
Chocolate mousse   Apple royale

*

Coffee

*

Recommended wines

Mouton Cadet Rouge   Mateus Rose

Babb's Pepsi's Executive Dining Room buffet

Chilled soursop nectar

*

Selection of local fruits

*

Ham and split pea soup
Chilled grapefruit consommé

*

Fillet of flying fish Bajan style
Baked whole kingfish with tartare sauce
Savoury macaroni pie
Caribbean shrimp with sweet and sour sauce
Braised chicken legs with savoury rice
Roast baron of beef with Yorkshire pudding

*

Baked jacket potatoes
Buttered okras   Egg plant fritters
Christophene creole   Eddoe pudding
Assorted salads

*

Choice of sweets from the dessert table

*

Guava cheese   Dinner mints
Cheese board

*

Coffee

*

Recommended wines

Chateau Timberlay   Chablis
Chateau Duplessis

Babb's Caribbean buffet

Chilled tropical nectar

*

Selection of local fruits

*

Ham and split pea soup
Chilled cucumber and tomato soup

*

Fried fillet of flying fish with lime tips
Baked whole kingfish with tartare sauce
Macaroni and cheese pie
Caribbean shrimp curry with rice and condiments
Braised chicken legs with pineapple chunks
Roast baron of beef with Yorkshire pudding

*

Baked jacket potatoes
Steamed pumpkin   Okras and sauce
Christophene au gratin   Creamed yam

*

Assorted salads

*

Choice of Sweets from the dessert table

*

Cheese board   Dinner mints
Coffee

*

Recommended wines

Chateau Cheval Blanc   Auxex-Duresses
Rose d'Anjou

Dalton supreme dinner

Green peppers filled with savoury eggplant and a touch of garlic
(6 peppers)
Caribbean fruit cup with rum and honey dressing
Spiced ham mousse with mustard dressing
Bajan shrimp cocktail

*

Local fish chowder
Iced curry soup

*

Sautéed kingfish arawak with banana and pineapple
(6 lbs. kingfish steaks)
Spiced roast chicken with prune and rosemary stuffing
(4 lbs. chicken breasts)
Fine herbes omelette or plain omelette

*

A selection of vegetables

*

Mixed salad bowl

*

Desserts from the trolley

*

Coupe peach melba
Various ice cream

*

Coffee

*

Recommended wines

Chilean Riesling   Chateau de Selle
Sangre de Toro

Dalton manor dinner

Smoked salmon and capers
Banana and chopped nut salad
Curried shrimp profiteroles
(6 lbs. shrimp)
Artichoke bases with paté foie gras

*

Cream of pumpkin soup
Chilled gazpacho

*

Escalope of veal with eggplant, tomatoes and green peppers
(6 lbs. veal)
Roast Long Island duckling with rum and orange sauce
(3 ducks)
Grilled sirloin steak served with chopped shallots cooked
in butter and parsley
A herb omelette with cream and grated cheese
Cold baked ham and salad
Fresh local lobster grilled with butter

*

A selection of vegetables

*

Mixed salad bowl

*

Desserts from the trolley

*

Various ice creams   Coupe Barbados

*

Coffee

*

Recommended wines

Pinot Noir   Piesporter
Chateau de Selle

Babb's New Year's Eve menu

Caribbean fresh fruit cocktail soaked in rum
Smoked salmon with capers
Spaghetti Milanaise style
Musk melon with Parma ham
Devilled shrimps with brown rice

*

Clear turtle soup with cheese straws
Cream of asparagus soup
Chilled consomme Julienne
Gazpacho Andaluz

*

Trout meuniere with flaked almonds
Coquille St Jacques Mornay

*

Lobster Cardinal
Cornish game hen cooked in coconut milk with tarragon and saffron
Roast baron of beef carved to order and served with Yorkshire
pudding and Jug Jug
Paupiettes of veal with tomatoes, green peppers and garlic
Cold poached salmon and salad
Broccoli spears   Gingered carrots
Croquette potatoes   Minted new potatoes
Mixed salad bowl

*

Flaming plum pudding   Brandy soufflé
Glazed mandarin and orange flan   Lemon meringue pie
Cream caramel   Crêpes filled with cherries and cream

*

Petit fours
Cheese board   Dinner mints
Coffee

*

Recommended wines

Monopole Vintage   Mouton Cadet Rouge
Pinot Chardonnay   Chateau de Selle

Babb's Christmas special beef stroganoff

12 lbs. sirloin steak
dry thyme
black pepper
garlic salt
2 large glasses sherry
2 sticks of butter
1 tsp. kitchen bouquet
3 large onions (chopped)
1 bottle A–1 Sauce

1 tblsp. Worcestershire sauce
2 cans mushroom soup
1 large container sour cream
1 can mushrooms
2 jiggers of sherry
6 cubes of beef boullion
$\frac{1}{2}$ tsp. thyme
1 tsp. garlic salt
$\frac{1}{2}$ tsp. black pepper

Slice steak into thin strips. Put in a large bowl and add the next four ingredients. Mix well and marinade for 25 minutes.
Put meat in skillet over low flame. Add butter and kitchen bouquet. Cook meat until tender. Add the rest of the ingredients and cook until all ingredients are tender.
Serve with wild rice and a green tossed salad.

Soup: Lentil with diced Franks
Beverage: Chablis wine
Dessert: Fresh strawberries with brown sugar and sour cream.

Christmas pone

(made from sweet cassava)

2 cups of sugar
6 lbs. of cassava
2 coconuts
$\frac{1}{2}$ tsp. cinnamon
1 box of raisins (1$\frac{1}{2}$ cups)
1$\frac{1}{2}$ cups milk
$\frac{1}{4}$ tsp. ginger

2 tblsp. vanilla extract
2 sticks of butter
2 sticks of lard
2 jiggers of sherry
1 tsp. baking powder
$\frac{1}{2}$ cup of almonds

Grind cassava and coconut flesh together. Mix all ingredients together and bake in greased baking pan at 300°F for one hour. Bake to brown. After baking, sprinkle over a mixture of one tablespoon of spice and one tablespoon sugar.
Serve with whipped cream.

Beverage: Coffee

Babb's special coconut bread and ginger beer at Christmas time

Coconut Bread

5 lbs. flour	1 lb. raisins
3 dry coconuts	1 lb. mixed peel
4 lbs. sugar	1 tsp. cinnamon
$\frac{1}{2}$ cup cooking oil	$\frac{1}{4}$ tsp. salt
3 sticks lard	$\frac{1}{4}$ tsp. ground ginger
$\frac{1}{2}$ lb. butter	3 tsp. baking powder
$\frac{1}{2}$ bottle vanilla essence	

Mix all ingredients to make the dough. Grease baking pan and bake at 350°F until brown.

Ginger Beer

1 lb. fresh ginger	6 cloves
25 rice grains	10 cups water
4 lbs. sugar	

Grate ginger on rough side of skin, place in big jug with 4 cups of water. Add rice, place cover on top of jug and let it sit overnight. Add 4 lbs. sugar and 6 cups of water to the ginger. Strain the ingredients through cheesecloth into 2 equal sized containers and add 3 cloves to each. Cover and keep in refrigerator.

From Babb's kitchen

FIRST COURSE
Melon with prosciutto

Peel and cut one melon to serve eight people, removing seeds. Wrap two slices of prosciutto around each slice of melon. Place wedge of lemon on top of each melon.
Serve Stolichnaya on the side.

SECOND COURSE
Salad

3 bags of spinach
1 lb. bacon
3 hard boiled eggs
$\frac{1}{4}$ head of red cabbage
$\frac{1}{4}$ sweet green pepper

$\frac{1}{4}$ fresh cauliflower
$\frac{1}{2}$ cup raisins
2 stalks of celery
$\frac{1}{2}$ onion, sliced
3 carrots, grated

Dressing: Italian
Serve with white wine

Fresh poached salmon

1 cut onion
2 celery stalks, sliced

1 whole salmon, filleted
   (about 6 lbs. in weight)

Place in poacher with enough water to cover salmon – boil water first. Sprinkle over $\frac{1}{4}$ tsp. thyme, $\frac{1}{2}$ tsp. garlic salt, $\frac{1}{4}$ tsp. black pepper and let it boil for $\frac{3}{4}$ of an hour. Remove skin and cool.
Serve chilled

Sauce for salmon

2 cans cream of mushroom soup
$\frac{1}{2}$ lbs. sharp Cheddar cheese,
   grated

$\frac{1}{2}$ lb. butter
$\frac{1}{2}$ cup milk

Stir ingredients until blended and add another $\frac{1}{2}$ cup milk, 1 tbs. flour and 3 packets chicken bouillon.

Dinner à la chef Babb

FIRST COURSE
Cream of celery soup

SECOND COURSE
Chicken breasts with mushroom sauce

8 boned chicken breasts,
  cooked and chilled (see
  below)
2 heads cauliflower
2 cans green peas
2 cans peach halves, drained
3 lbs. fresh asparagus (use tips
  only)

2 lbs. Chedder cheese, cut into
  strips
1 large honeydew melon,
  peeled and sliced
1½ lbs. prosciutto ham, sliced
  thin and placed over melon
  slices

Cook chicken breasts with dried thyme, fresh onion, garlic salt, celery stalk. Simmer for one hour or until tender.
Arrange chicken on platter over lettuce and decorate with other ingredients. Add mushroom cheese sauce just before serving or serve separately. Serves 8.

Mushroom cheese sauce

¼ cup grated onion
½ lb. Cheddar cheese, grated
1 cup milk
½ lb. butter

2 pkges. chicken bouillon
  powder
2 cans cream of mushroom soup
1 dstsp. flour

Place milk and butter in skillet and simmer gently. Add cream of mushroom soup, flour, chicken bouillon, and grated cheese. Stir gently and cook about 25 minutes. Chill before serving. Sauce may be thinned with additional milk if too thick.
Serve with a white wine, preferably a Chablis.

THIRD COURSE
Chef Babb's strawberry dessert

5 pints fresh strawberries $\frac{1}{2}$ cup brown sugar
$1\frac{1}{2}$ pints sour cream

Wash and pick over strawberries thoroughly. Drain well. Mix brown sugar with berries. Place sour cream over berries and stir gently. Serve chilled.

Chicken à la Bagshot Hotel

2 whole chickens   1 tsp. sugar
2 large onions   raisins to taste
1 large stalk celery   dry parsley flakes
thyme   1 bottle chutney
$\frac{1}{2}$ cup butter   Tabasco sauce to taste
3 tsp. curry powder   salt
2 sweet peppers   pepper
$\frac{1}{2}$ can tomato puree

To prepare chickens, cook (whole or in parts) in large pot with water to which is added thyme, salt, pepper, one large onion (sliced), and $\frac{1}{2}$ stalk celery; cook until chicken is tender, about one hour. Bone chicken, cut in small pieces and set aside.

In a large pot, sauté one chopped onion, rest of celery and two sweet peppers for about 20 minutes, in butter, until tender. Add the rest of the ingredients and the chicken pieces; cook until thoroughly heated, about 20 minutes. Serve with condiments; bananas, raisins, coconut, peanuts (chopped) and more chutney. Serves 6.

(This recipe is better when prepared the day before it is served, and refrigerated.)

Suggested wine: Marques de Murrieta
Soup: Cream of Spinach

Babb's Thanksgiving dinner

1 whole turkey, medium size
  (with gizzard)
3 lbs. pork sausage
juice from $1\frac{1}{2}$ lemons
3 sticks butter
2 bags herb stuffing mix
1 onion. minced very fine
4 sticks celery, chopped
$\frac{1}{2}$ cup white cooking wine
$1\frac{1}{2}$ tsp. salt
$1\frac{1}{2}$ tsp. thyme
2 tsp. black pepper
$\frac{1}{2}$ tsp. garlic powder
$\frac{1}{2}$ tsp. chicken poultry
  seasoning

$\frac{1}{2}$ tsp. dry mustard
2 tsp. seasoned salt
8 large baking potatoes,
  unpeeled
1 stick butter
$\frac{1}{2}$ onion, grated
$\frac{1}{4}$ tsp. thyme
$\frac{1}{4}$ tsp. white pepper
$\frac{1}{4}$ cup milk
2 tsp. catsup
1 whole cauliflower
1 stick butter
$\frac{1}{2}$ cup flour
$\frac{1}{2}$ cup milk
salt and pepper to taste

Place the turkey in a roasting pan. Add one teaspoon of salt to the lemon juice and rub turkey thoroughly with this mixture and let stand for 30 minutes. While turkey is standing, prepare stuffing. In a large skillet, melt all of the butter, adding onion, celery and $\frac{1}{2}$ teaspoon of black pepper. While this mixture is being sautéed, chop one pound of the sausage and the turkey gizzard and add to the skillet. Also add the stuffing mix and wine and slowly cook.

Wash the turkey inside and out after letting it stand 30 minutes. Rub the outside with one teaspoon salt. Inside the turkey, sprinkle a mixture of one teaspoon each of thyme, black pepper and salt. When the stuffing mix is ready, place inside the turkey. Grease the roasting pan and cover turkey with aluminum foil and roast at 400°F for approximately two hours, depending on its size. After cooking for $1\frac{1}{2}$ hours, reduce oven to 300°F and remove foil and baste turkey with drippings. While turkey is browning, cook the remaining two pounds of pork sausage and when turkey is placed on serving platter, surround with this sausage.

As turkey is cooking, boil potatoes. When thoroughly cooked, halve the potatoes lengthwise. Scoop out the potato from the skin and set skins aside. Place potatoes in a bowl. In a skillet, melt one stick of butter and add to it half of the onion, and $\frac{1}{4}$ teaspoon each of thyme and white pepper. Add this mixture to potatoes, adding $\frac{1}{4}$ cup milk. Whip very lightly, and stuff each potato back into its skin. On top of each one, place a dab of catsup. Place potatoes in oven while turkey is cooking and brown about 20 minutes.

While turkey is roasting, boil cauliflower whole. When tender, season to taste with salt and pepper. In a skillet or small pot, melt one stick of butter and stir in $\frac{1}{2}$ cup of flour and add, slowly, $\frac{1}{2}$ cup milk, stirring constantly. Just before serving, pour cream sauce over the cauliflower.

Serve with Monsieur Henri's Cartier Sauvignon Blanc.

Keep Cool American platter

Place lettuce on platter
Roast beef, sliced and chilled
Ham
American Cheese
Swiss Cheese
Liverwurst
Bologna
Fresh mushrooms
Fresh strawberries

Salami
Sliced tomatoes
Sliced cucumbers
Bermuda onions
Green and black olives
Carrot sticks
Celery
Radishes
Apple Sauce
White and Rye breads

Your guest can either have this as a sandwich or cold platter. Serve with Thousand Island dressing, blue cheese, mustard or mayonnaise.

Soup: Gazpacho
Beverage: Iced Tea, Lemonade, Pepsi.

Babb's St Croix special

Use either fresh fillet of cod or striped bass.

Soak fish in pan with two squeezed lemons and sprinkled salt for 25 minutes. Wash fish off and add 1 large onion, sliced.

Place onion on bottom of pan and lay fish on top. Cover fish with another sliced onion and four fresh sliced tomatoes.

Sprinkle with black pepper, garlic salt, dry thyme.
Add 1 stick of butter.
Squeeze 1 whole lemon over fish.
Add 3 dashes of tabasco sauce, 4 chicken flavoured bouillon, 1 small can of tomato paste.
Cover with foil and steam about 35 minutes.
Serve with rice and tossed green salad

Soup: Seafood Gumbo
Dessert: Fresh Fruit Salad
Beverage: Iced tea or Coffee

Babb's special diet

Lettuce

Carrots

Cucumber

Cottage cheese

Broccoli

Cauliflower

Celery

Parsley

Sweet red peppers

Oranges

Melba toast

American cheese

Tea with lemon, no sugar

High blood pressure menu

	1,200 calories	1,800 calories	Unrestricted calories
Breakfast	½ cup orange juice poached egg on toast coffee or tea	½ grapefruit ½ cup oatmeal 2 tbsp. cream coffee or tea	¼ cantaloupe scrambled egg toast unsalted butter coffee or tea

Lunch	¼ cup cottage
	   cheese with
	   lettuce and
	   tomato
	½ cup green beans
	1 slice bread
	peach slices
	1 cup milk
		3 oz. hamburger pattie
		green salad
		2 tbsp. French
		   dressing
		½ cup cauliflower
		1 roll
		1 tsp. unsalted
		   butter
		pear
		1 cup milk
			¼ cup dietetic
			   tunafish on lettuce
			unsalted mayon-
			   naise
			½ cup asparagus
			1 slice bread
			unsalted butter
			12 grapes
			1 cup milk

Dinner	3 oz. roast pork
	1 small potato
	¼ acorn squash
	1 roll
	½ cup apple sauce
	1 cup skim milk
	(add 2 tsp. unsalted
	   fat to meal)
		3 oz. baked chicken
		   leg
		½ cup rice
		½ cup peas
		1 biscuit
		2 tsp. unsalted
		   butter
		½ cup pineapple
		1 cup milk
			3 oz. roast beef
			baked potato
			½ cup broccoli
			1 roll
			unsalted butter
			cherry pie
			1 cup milk

Snack	(Bedtime or between meals) Fruit	Fruit	Fruit